Mindfulness Workbook

Learn From Tibetan Monks How You Can Live a Happy

(Easy Meditation Techniques to Reduce Stress, Anxiety and Conflict and Instantly Feel Better)

Luis Boucher

Published by Rob Miles

© **Luis Boucher**

All Rights Reserved

Mindfulness Workbook: Learn From Tibetan Monks How You Can Live a Happy (Easy Meditation Techniques to Reduce Stress, Anxiety and Conflict and Instantly Feel Better)

ISBN 978-1-989990-94-0

All rights reserved. No part of this guide may be reproduced in any form without permission in writing from the publisher except in the case of brief quotations embodied in critical articles or reviews.

Legal & Disclaimer

The information contained in this book is not designed to replace or take the place of any form of medicine or professional medical advice. The information in this book has been provided for educational and entertainment purposes only.

The information contained in this book has been compiled from sources deemed reliable, and it is accurate to the best of the Author's knowledge; however, the Author cannot guarantee its accuracy and validity and cannot be held liable for any errors or omissions. Changes are periodically made to this book. You must consult your doctor or get professional medical advice before using any of the suggested remedies, techniques, or information in this book.

Upon using the information contained in this book, you agree to hold harmless the Author from and against any damages, costs, and expenses, including any legal fees potentially resulting from the application of any of the information provided by this guide. This disclaimer applies to any damages or injury caused by the use and application, whether directly or indirectly, of any advice or information presented, whether for breach of contract, tort, negligence, personal injury, criminal intent, or under any other cause of action.

You agree to accept all risks of using the information presented inside this book. You need to consult a professional medical practitioner in order to ensure you are both able and healthy enough to participate in this program.

Table of Contents

INTRODUCTION 1

CHAPTER 1: WHAT IS MINDFULNESS? 3

CHAPTER 2: HOW TO START BEING MINDFUL 16

CHAPTER 3: THE "CONSTANT CHANGE" MEDITATION 27

CHAPTER 4: PRECISELY, WHY HAVE WE WRITTEN THIS BOOK? 43

CHAPTER 5: MINDFULNESS METHODS AND MINDFULNESS MEDITATION 48

CHAPTER 6: BREATHING EXERCISES TECHNIQUE 63

CHAPTER 7: TIPS FOR SUCCESS 67

CHAPTER 8: SHIFTING OUT OF NEGATIVE SPACE 73

CHAPTER 9: FOUR NOBLE TRUTHS 80

CHAPTER 10: MEDITATION FOR BETTER SLEEP 89

CHAPTER 11: THOUGHT AWARENESS 93

CHAPTER 12: WAYS TO BE MINDFUL AT WORK 97

CHAPTER 13: DEALING WITH DISTRACTIONS WHILE MEDITATING 102

CHAPTER 14: MINDFULNESS CAN IMPROVE YOUR RELATIONSHIPS 106

CHAPTER 15: MINDFULNESS CAN IMPROVE YOUR RELATIONSHIPS 113

- CHAPTER 16: THOUGHTS ARE NOT FACTS 119
- CHAPTER 17: GUIDE TO PRACTICING THE MEDITATION. 132
- CHAPTER 18: EXTERNAL WORLD AND BREATH TECHNIQUE 140
- CHAPTER 19: MINDFULNESS IN YOUR DAILY LIFE 143
- CHAPTER 20: LOVING KINDNESS 148
- CHAPTER 21: MINDFULNESS AND RELATIONSHIPS 161
- CHAPTER 22: POSITIVE MIND, POSITIVE LIFE 181
- CONCLUSION 190

Introduction

How is your typical Monday-Friday? Do you get up early each day and spend nearly every working hour pre-occupied with work? Do you have to wade through an onslaught of meetings, keep appointments and generally handle responsibility after responsibility until it is time to go home? There's nothing wrong with any of this; in fact, most Americans live this way, and it enables them to pay their bills, take care of their own, and set their kids up for even brighter futures.

However, such a lifestyle often undermines mindfulness. You go through each week like a drone or robot, performing tasks on autopilot and never really being "in the moment." And in doing so, you never really get to enjoy all that life has to offer.

This book will teach you more about mindfulness. It will show you what to do so that you savor each moment and truly enjoy life. It will help you retreat from the hamster wheel of our "go-go-go" society, which (wrongly) glorifies being busy, and working hard over being mindful and deliberate in your actions.

Thanks again for purchasing this book. I hope you enjoy it!

Chapter 1: What Is Mindfulness?

I have touched on what mindfulness is without actually spelling it out for you so far. Mindfulness is being aware of the very moment that you are in. We go through our lives and we are often absent from them. Our thoughts are elsewhere. We may be on the way to work, but thinking about something the kids said as they went out to school. We may be performing our first task at work, but thinking about how we would love to be back in bed. Retrospective thought and thoughts about the future are excluded when you step into a mindfulness session and whether that session comprises 10 or even 5 minutes, it's adding value to your life, because you are actually living it. The Dalai Lama was once asked what amazed him about mankind.

If you take this literally, it means that for every hour of your life, you may only be conscious of a few seconds of what it actually happening with your time. You may be present in your life, but you are not really aware. How many times have you driven somewhere and not remembered the journey? We all do this but when you make it a habit to practice mindfulness, you place yourself in the moment and no matter what you are doing, this is possible.

For example, when you get out of bed in the morning, what are your first thoughts? Try to think to yourself that the day is ready to greet you and become aware of the way the light plays into the room through the gaps in the drapes, or how the world looks different with different types of weather. You should never let this get you down, but embrace the changes and challenges presented to you through your life in the moment, rather than worrying about future or past. I once opened the drapes in my room and was confronted with the most amazing rainbow I have ever witnessed. It kind of reminded me of why I greet the day and on that particular day, I was particularly happy that it was raining but that the sun had managed to escape from behind the clouds to cause that array of color that greeted me with optimism and hope. Most of the time we go through our lives with our eyes closed off to the things that can make the most difference to our lives, because ... our minds are too occupied elsewhere.

Exercise 1 in Mindfulness

You need to get up and get your breakfast. As you get out of bed, tell yourself that you are happy it is another day. Be aware of the sensations of your body. Be aware of the movements of your limbs and breathe consciously so that you are in the breath at the same time as you are getting ready to face the world. Be aware of your surroundings. Be aware of what you are dressed in and what you are going to get dressed in. Be in the moment and enjoy the breath.

What you are doing in this moment of mindfulness is allowing yourself to live that moment of your life instead of ignoring it in favor of thoughts from other times. Of course, thoughts will enter your head from time to time, but acknowledge them and then let them go if they do not relate to the moment that you are celebrating in your life.

The same exercise can be applied to eating and drinking, taking in the flavors and scents of your food and chewing it thoroughly so that you are aware of the textures and tastes. It can also apply to menial tasks that you may not enjoy doing. The fact is that if you immerse yourself into the moment and concentrate on what needs to be done, you will do it faster and more effectively without all the negative thoughts about not wanting to do it. Try it on your next housework. Breathe and be conscious of the breath and be aware of your body movements as you go about the task. Be aware of your stance and your effort. Applaud your effort while getting the job done and use this time to breathe and to be in the moment.

In a work situation, you may have some jobs that are more difficult than others. In this case scenario, the ideal is to use mindfulness by trying to find a place where you will not be disturbed. Switch off the phone, place an answering email in service while you do the tasks that you have prioritized as being important. Don't let distraction pull you away from what you have to do and live each moment actually present in what you are doing, being aware of your body posture, your breath, your limb movements and the way your brain works its way through the task in an orderly manner until the task is done. If the task is too big, break it down into manageable chunks and work on one at a time so that you achieve the same thing. Being mindful of the greater good as well as mindful of the thoughts that sneak into your head, you are able to take control of this moment in your life and perform more efficiently.

Mindfulness doesn't mean extra effort. It means simply being where you are at the given time and being aware of your surroundings, your body and your breathing and taking advantage of that moment of your life that you may otherwise have lost. If you look back on your last hour, how much of that time was spent mindfully? The chances are that very little of it was. Try to control your thought processes by telling thoughts that unless they actually relate to this moment, it's the wrong time for you to think about them. Imagine the thought being a balloon and banish it by popping the balloon. Mindfulness is being aware. That's all it is, but if you take a look around you and keep a note of things that people say to you during the course of one day, you will find that not very many people are actually in the moment at all. Some may talk about past experiences. Some may give in to worries about the future. You need to exercise your mindfulness on a regular basis so that it becomes your norm rather than the exception. That way you get more value out of your life and are happier and healthier because of it.

Remember in the first chapter, I told you about the origins of mindfulness meditation and drew out the plan that the Original Buddha had for mankind. Mindfulness was one of the steps toward getting away from your suffering and is noted in the Eightfold Path, but there are other things that are equally important to your mindfulness that were shown as being part of the eightfold path. Try to include these in your life and your way of thinking and you will find that mindfulness and meditation enriches who you are and how you relate to the world around you.

Exercise 2 in Mindfulness

For this exercise, I want you to write down the list of the eightfold path items. It only has to be a small list, but keep it with you where you can refer to it all day long. If you are being mindful about your life, then the chances are that you are already doing the things on that list, but relate it to your life. Look at whether you are being kind to others, saying the right things, doing the right things and being mindful of your life in this very moment in time. All of these rules contribute toward your happiness and if you get something wrong on that list, don't beat yourself up about it. Simply acknowledge it and move on. You will find that you become more present in your life and that you start to take responsibility for your own happiness. You are not as negative as you were and do not place blame on people when things go wrong. You will also find that jealousy is something you can put to one side because you now acknowledge that we are all separate and that our reality is not always the reality of others. Be compassionate with yourself and with others.

Learn the Eightfold Path by heart and try to stick to it during the course of your day. Tick those items that you know you excelled at and celebrate your ability to understand how YOU affect your state of happiness, rather than it being the responsibility of others or of outside influences. We are all responsible for the emotions that we feel. The reason why mindfulness is so powerful is because it reinforces your meditation practice and when you have the two elements in place in your life, life gets to be more positive and happy. People say that happiness is elusive but the fact is that it's always been there. Perhaps you were not looking in the right places or were lacking in observation of the potential of happiness. Mindfulness teaches you the joy of this moment, no matter how menial a task you have to perform. In fact, one of the favorite tasks of students in ashrams all over the world is actually cleaning the floor. It helps to level off their ego at the same time as showing them that no matter how lowly the task, being mindful about doing it gives much pleasure and allows them to enjoy the moment. It helps to silence the mind if you can take on these tasks with humility and simply be in the moment while you perform them. By opening your eyes and all your senses to the potential of your life, you forget about being insular and unhappy. The stress factor is less pronounced and you are able to find joy in even the smallest of things. I remember one student gazing at the water draining away from her bucket. She had never thought to look before, but seeing it swirling around in circles and disappearing down the drain, she said it was almost like feeling her own negativity draining away while she had been cleaning the floor. The one habit that she had always found hard to get rid of was multitasking. She had this idea that it paid off dividends to multi-task but when we analyzed it, what we both found was not only can the brain not concentrate properly on two things, but neither of those things gives you the same satisfaction or is performed as well as when concentrating solely on one task.

Exercise 3 – Mindfulness in nature

There is a lot to be said about using nature as a wonderful inspiration in your life. You see the trees in winter lose their leaves and the world becomes very cold, but isn't it absolutely amazing that in the springtime, all of the trees will start to begin their cycle again and the buds will become new and start the cycle of life over again? It's a wonderful thing to notice and to use the senses on. For this exercise, I would simply ask that you observe nature more during your life. Look at how things change and grow and if you would like to, you can even begin to grow something yourself. A thing as simple as a carrot top can produce the most amazing foliage and all you need to do is to place it into a saucer of water.

Meditation takes you within yourself, but it also changes the way that you relate to the world around you. Thus, you begin to notice the changes of the seasons or the growth on plants, the flowers and the changes in weather and also see a positive change in embracing life. Walk often in an environment that is natural and be aware of sights and sounds. It may even help you to keep a diary of these weekly visits to a place that makes you feel peaceful. You may even just be taking the dog for a walk. It doesn't have to be anything difficult to include in your life. The difference is that you approach it with complete presence and use all of your senses to enjoy whatever it is that you choose to do. One of the problems that mankind is suffering from in this day and age is information overload, to the extent that we no longer listen to our intuition. As you get more and more involved in meditation, you will be very surprised that your intuition becomes stronger, but it's not because there are actual changes physiologically – even though some changes do occur. It's because you are more aware of yourself and your surroundings and are therefore better able to tune into your intuition.

I read a criminology book that explained what happens in a busy world when you do not listen to the intuition and are distracted from taking notice of what your mind is trying to tell you. Although the cases in question were a little extreme, it was worth noting that often the mind and body are trying to tell you things and these may relate to your inner workings or to the way the world around you is posing any kind of threat. Intuition is a tool to help you to perceive yourself, your inner workings and to be able to protect you against things that you may otherwise not have noticed. Your journey into awareness will help you to develop better instincts that in turn help you to become happier and safer in your life. It is a good idea to switch off the noise of the world sometimes and simply be, which is why meditation is so valuable.

Chapter 2: How To Start Being Mindful

So that's mindfulness essentially, the following question is how you start applying it.

One possibility is to utilize online 'guided meditations.' These are basically audios that direct you on what to do as you attempt meditating. For instance, they might inform you to shut your eyes and breathe in and out throughout the nose.

Then they could inform you to contemplate your body. One especially good resource that accomplishes this is the Headspace App which can be downloaded for Android or iOS but which is likewise available to utilize via the web. This will talk you through various directed meditations, but only the initial ten are cost-free. Still, you can discover enough from those ten sessions to then flourish without the app.

Generally, though, the majority of mindfulness meditations will take a very identical method and you can undergo the steps then without essentially having to be talked through it. And as a matter of fact, if you can do your meditation without instruction, then you ought to find that you're in fact more successful at it due to the fact that you won't be constantly interrupted by someone's voice.

Let's discuss what the steps will typically be for a mindfulness meditation program.

Step 1: Breathing

The primary thing to do is to begin breathing. You can do this utilizing something referred to as 'equal breathing' from yoga. Here, you inhale through the nose and out through the mouth. As you accomplish this, you retain each inhalation and exhalation for 3 seconds. These lengthy draws in and lengthy exhalations will enable you to entirely fill up the lungs with clean oxygen and eliminate all the CO_2.

But to be truthful, you can use any sort of breathing so long as it is gradual, intentional and full. The direction they give on the Headspace App, for example, is just to 'breathe loud enough so that the individual beside you would manage to hear.'

Why breathing? Basically, breathing gradually is the ideal way to signal to the body that the coast is clear and you're secure. We breathe rapidly when we're worried to get more air around our bodies and we can inhale more slowly when we are calm. Therefore, breathing deeply and gradually will aid us to leave the 'fight or flight' state and to enter the 'rest and digest' state alternatively. This ought to correct our heart rate variance, decrease cortisol and get us prepared to go into a relaxed state.

Step 2: Senses

Next, you are frequently told to pay attention to your physical senses. This implies observing the smells, sounds and also the temperature throughout the room. Your eyes will typically be closed, so sight is dismissed from this one.

The goal here is not to 'search' for sounds or attempt to hear them. Rather, just observe the sounds that you don't typically. You might discover that you can hear squeaking in the house, perhaps you can hear the next-door neighbors, perhaps you can hear the rain outdoors or the wind.There are possibly far off birds and/or traffic.

This is often a great example of just how little we typically focus on and how much richer our experience ends up being when we engage in mindfulness. It's likewise a fantastic way to get involved in that habit and to begin unwinding the body even more.

Step 3: Body Scan

Body scan meditation is in some cases referred to as being its own thing, but it could be used as a component of any meditation session. The concept here is just to become more mindful of your own body as we explained earlier but to accomplish this by methodically starting on top of the head and after that moving progressively through to the toes, observing how you feel at every stage.

If you wish to use this procedure to get to sleep, at that point, it could be a fantastic tool for that objective too. The ideal way to accomplish this, though, is to make an effort to completely relax the muscles by initially contracting and then releasing each portion of your body as you go through it. What you'll discover is that you hold big amounts of tension all over from your face muscles, to your neck, to your limbs. Once you acknowledge this and let it go, you'll feel much more relaxed and ultimately, this can allow you to enter deep and restful sleep.

In the meantime, though, we're just examining the body and utilizing this as a method to end up being more mindful of our own selves and to start the procedure of introspection and self-directed attention.

Step 4: Concentrate On Breathing

After observing each part of the body, go back to the chest and pay specific focus to the way it fluctuates. As you accomplish this, you can likewise take this chance to correct your breathing.

Odds are, that when you first observe your own breathing, you'll discover that you are breathing in so that your chest broadens initially. But actually, it ought to be your abdomen that moves initially and this ought to after that be followed by your chest. Appropriate breathing (called abdominal breathing) ought to start by enabling the stomach to loosen up and stick out and then filling the lungs.

This is helpful because the process creates space in your abdominal cavity. This at that point, enables the lungs to expand into that space, which is after that followed by them extending upwards through your chest too.

This kind of breathing permits you to ingest more oxygen and to, thus, activate even more pleasure hormones. The majority of us don't use this type of breathing though due to the fact that we have hunched postures which tuck our stomach and hinder us from managing to breathe from there. The outcome is that we wind up breathing with much shallower and quicker breaths, which in fact raises stress and cortisol.

But don't stress over that if you don't wish to. In the meantime, just observe your own breath and take this chance to count your breaths as they come in and out. This is the portion that is going to function a bit like transcendental meditation by silencing a great deal of the activity across the brain.

Step 5: Allow Your Mind to Wander

Once you've accomplished this for a little while and you're feeling especially calm, it's time just to free your mind and allow it to do whatever it desires. Now your goal is not to attempt and control or silence your thoughts. Rather, you just let your mind stray naturally or to remain entirely still if it wishes to.

The explanation that is frequently used is that you're 'monitoring thoughts proceed like clouds'. Headspace defines your thoughts in these instances as being more like cars in the street. It highlights the importance of viewing the 'cars' pass by but not going out into the road to go after the traffic. This is all about detached monitoring.

After you have accomplished this for some time, you can just allow your thoughts to slowly return to normal and lightly open your eyes.

Tips for Fast Improvement

A great deal of people try to begin meditating, but they wind up falling short. Why is this?

One issue is that a lot of us wish to get instant results and want to feel immediately different. When this doesn't occur, we wind up annoyed and stressed. This is the nastiest mindset you can perhaps take to mindfulness meditation. The entire point is that you are to allow your mind do whatever it desires. As soon as you begin pushing it in one direction or another, you are going to drop that all-important freedom and begin generating stress hormones.

Also, attempt not to get too disturbed with yourself if you attempt this and your brain keeps straying or you keep getting sidetracked. If you get itchy, it's okay to scratch your skin. If you require a glass of water, stand up and get one. Don't attempt and pressure anything; just allow yourself to 'be' as you are truly.

If you truly want assistance jump-starting your progress though, at that point, you ought to think about 'priming' yourself. Priming is a terminology used in psychology that just pertains to prepping the brain in a particular way.

In some cases, that means affecting the responses we provide to questions by presenting a certain stimulus. But in other instances, it means altering our emotions. In this case, it pays to perform anything calming, but that, nonetheless, calls for concentration just before you attempt meditating.

So, for instance, you could attempt relaxing in a lovely but novel location. Novel scenery boost neurotransmitters and hormones connected with concentration, while being in natural surroundings has been shown to make us more loosened up and to stimulate slower brainwaves.

Lastly, don't be too aggressive relative to how frequently you plan to meditate. Another traditional error is to set out with the plan that you're going to meditate for 30 minutes each day. This is doomed to for fail unless you presently devoting 30 minutes of each day bored out of your head. Begin with something modest-- even just 5 minutes prior to waking up and afterward, you can improve this habit.

Chapter 3: The "Constant Change" Meditation

Everything around is constantly changing, forever evolving. Just think about the 4 seasons of nature, the alternation between day and night or the unstoppable rhythm of time. You see, when we have a scar in our soul due to a past event, we tend to think that it will be with us for the rest of time. This would be true if we were static creatures, but being created by nature we follow the universal law of evolution.

Everything is evolving on a large and small scale. On a large scale, we started our evolution millions of years ago, when the first organic cells started forming. On a small scale, each and everyone of us goes through a personal evolution, that goes from the moment they were born to the moment of their death. Well, actually some traditions and cultures believes that the journey does not begin or end with life, but that is outside our interest for the time being.

What is important to understand, in order to really grasp the benefits of this practice, is that what we feel today will not last forever, even if we think so. This goes for good and bad feelings, without distinctions. I know that if you have just gone through a difficult period of your life, you might think you will never fully recover. I hope this practice will give you that extra hope that it is possible and that you are already on the path to happiness.

Let's get started!

Find a comfortable, relaxed and balanced position. Give yourself permission to be completely present for yourself, and let your body and mind calm down until they become soft and relaxed.

Breathe in, feel relaxed...

breathe out, feel calm...

Breathe in, feel relaxed...

breathe out, feel calm...

Breathe in, feel relaxed...

breathe out, feel calm...

Breathe in, feel relaxed...

breathe out, feel calm...

Allow the mind to distance itself from all thoughts and orientate awareness on your breath. Breathe naturally and do not force a specific rhythm. Let your breath come and go.

Carefully, now, drive your attention from the breath to the space in which you are.

Feel the energy and atmosphere of this space as it permeates all of your being. Notice the noises in the background. Maybe there is a clock ticking, maybe there are cars passing just outside your windows. Whatever you feel it is fine, let your attention rest on the external.

Breathe in, feel relaxed...

breathe out, feel calm...

Breathe in, feel relaxed...

breathe out, feel calm...

Breathe in, feel relaxed...

breathe out, feel calm...

Breathe in, feel relaxed...

breathe out, feel calm...

Now bring the attention back to the breath. Take your time and you will naturally reach a place of warmth and ease. Stay in this state where you feel your body and mind completely calm, relaxed and full of peace for a few minutes, without letting go the focus on your breath.

Breathe in, feel relaxed...

breathe out, feel calm...

Breathe in, feel relaxed...

breathe out, feel calm...

Breathe in, feel relaxed...

breathe out, feel calm...

Breathe in, feel relaxed...

breathe out, feel calm...

Breathe in, feel relaxed...

breathe out, feel calm...

Breathe in, feel relaxed...

breathe out, feel calm...

Breathe in, feel relaxed...

breathe out, feel calm...

Breathe in, feel relaxed...

breathe out, feel calm...

Now that you have reached this deep sense of relaxation, we can begin to shift our focus to the present moment. Allow your mind to naturally sink deeper into the layers of thoughts, until you can start observing everything from a third person perspective.

I will give you a few minutes to do that, as it might take some time for some of you.

Breathe in, feel relaxed...

breathe out, feel calm...

Breathe in, feel relaxed...

breathe out, feel calm...

Breathe in, feel relaxed...

breathe out, feel calm...

Breathe in, feel relaxed...

breathe out, feel calm...

Breathe in, feel relaxed...

breathe out, feel calm...

Breathe in, feel relaxed...

breathe out, feel calm...

Breathe in, feel relaxed...

breathe out, feel calm...

Breathe in, feel relaxed...

breathe out, feel calm...

As you now can see yourself from above, keep following the present moment, grasping everything happening externally and internally. All the emotions arising, all the noises in the background: everything has the same importance and it is worth noticing.

Breathe in, feel relaxed...

breathe out, feel calm...

Breathe in, feel relaxed...

breathe out, feel calm...

Breathe in, feel relaxed...

breathe out, feel calm...

Breathe in, feel relaxed...

breathe out, feel calm...

You may soon realize that everything that comes under your attention, sooner or later leaves your field of mental contact, as something else enters it. This is something worth noting and I will give you a couple of minutes to realize this, as it is the main concept of the entire practice.

Breathe in, feel relaxed...

breathe out, feel calm...

Breathe in, feel relaxed...

breathe out, feel calm...

Breathe in, feel relaxed...

breathe out, feel calm...

Breathe in, feel relaxed...

breathe out, feel calm...

What before was here, now it is not any more and it the space that it created, something else if coming in to fill in the gap. Do not resist the constant and progressive evolution of what you are feeling and perceiving, as it the most basic law of the universe presenting itself to you in its most natural form.

Breathe in, feel relaxed...

breathe out, feel calm...

Breathe in, feel relaxed...

breathe out, feel calm...

Breathe in, feel relaxed...

breathe out, feel calm...

Breathe in, feel relaxed...

breathe out, feel calm...

Breathe in, feel relaxed...

breathe out, feel calm...

Breathe in, feel relaxed...

breathe out, feel calm...

Breathe in, feel relaxed...

breathe out, feel calm...

Breathe in, feel relaxed...

breathe out, feel calm...

The same way noise come and go, the same way your thoughts constantly change, your scars will heal and make place for new beauty and peace. You just need to give yourself time and allow the healing process to take place, without resisting it with your mind.

You do not have to do anything, besides allowing the natural evolution to take place in its most natural form. Evolving means being ready to let go of what no longer serves you and when you will reach the point where you can allow your scars to truly heal, than pain will make space for new positive energy.

Breathe in, feel relaxed...

breathe out, feel calm...

Breathe in, feel relaxed...

breathe out, feel calm...

Breathe in, feel relaxed...

breathe out, feel calm...

Breathe in, feel relaxed...

breathe out, feel calm...

Breathe in, feel relaxed...

breathe out, feel calm...

Breathe in, feel relaxed...

breathe out, feel calm...

Breathe in, feel relaxed...

breathe out, feel calm...

Breathe in, feel relaxed...

breathe out, feel calm...

Just keep noticing everything that goes on inside and outside you. It can be useful to label each thing with a name. For example, whenever you feel a thought arising, you can say "thought" inside your head. This will help you look at things from a third person perspective, without judging what you are feeling.

Breathe in, feel relaxed...

breathe out, feel calm...

Breathe in, feel relaxed...

breathe out, feel calm...

Breathe in, feel relaxed...

breathe out, feel calm...

Breathe in, feel relaxed...

breathe out, feel calm...

Breathe in, feel relaxed...

breathe out, feel calm...

Breathe in, feel relaxed...

breathe out, feel calm...

Breathe in, feel relaxed...

breathe out, feel calm...

Breathe in, feel relaxed...

breathe out, feel calm...

Keep noticing and labelling, as this process reinforces the idea that everything is here to go away and that change is the only true constant. Now you have thoughts, now you have noises, now you are scared, now you have courage. It is a never ending cycle of "things" and we are here to witness this marvellous show unfolding in front of our very own eyes.

Breathe in, feel relaxed...

breathe out, feel calm...

Breathe in, feel relaxed...

breathe out, feel calm...

Breathe in, feel relaxed...

breathe out, feel calm...

Breathe in, feel relaxed...

breathe out, feel calm...

Breathe in, feel relaxed...

breathe out, feel calm...

Breathe in, feel relaxed...

breathe out, feel calm...

Breathe in, feel relaxed...

breathe out, feel calm...

Breathe in, feel relaxed...

breathe out, feel calm...

I will give you a few more minutes to focus on this, before reaching the end of our session.

Breathe in, feel relaxed...

breathe out, feel calm...

Breathe in, feel relaxed...

breathe out, feel calm...

Breathe in, feel relaxed...

breathe out, feel calm...

Breathe in, feel relaxed...

breathe out, feel calm...
Breathe in, feel relaxed...
breathe out, feel calm...
Breathe in, feel relaxed...
breathe out, feel calm...
Breathe in, feel relaxed...
breathe out, feel calm...
Breathe in, feel relaxed...
breathe out, feel calm...
Breathe in, feel relaxed...
breathe out, feel calm...
Breathe in, feel relaxed...
breathe out, feel calm...
Breathe in, feel relaxed...
breathe out, feel calm...
Breathe in, feel relaxed...

breathe out, feel calm...

Breathe in, feel relaxed...

breathe out, feel calm...

Breathe in, feel relaxed...

breathe out, feel calm...

Breathe in, feel relaxed...

breathe out, feel calm...

Now bring the attention back to the body and start feeling your arms and legs once again. You can close your hands or move your fingers, just to take control of the space around you.

Please, keep the eyes closed for now and enjoy the beautiful moment you are living. You have given yourself the time to feel better and that is absolutely incredible.

Breathe in, feel relaxed...

breathe out, feel calm...

Breathe in, feel relaxed...

breathe out, feel calm...

Breathe in, feel relaxed...

breathe out, feel calm...

Breathe in, feel relaxed...

breathe out, feel calm...

Now become aware of the environment around you once again. Feel the different sounds, the temperature of the room you are in and once you are ready, open the eyes again.

Chapter 4: Precisely, Why Have We Written This Book?

We published the book since we were aware of its enormous advantage. We published it out of our genuine desire to help. Many paths led us to these objectives. Here, we would love to talk about ourselves and the journey of ours.

We have devoted a great portion of our work to the understanding, causes as well as treatment of anxiety and anxiety disorders. Much more broadly, we're united in our aim to discover much better methods to relieve human suffering by cultivating mental health and wellness. We focused on helping individuals gain control and mastery over their distressing feelings and thoughts using many methods, many of which provided "new, various, better" means to replace thoughts and feelings. You most likely know about this method. Perhaps you have discovered the right way to determine catastrophic negative feelings to see they're impractical and then to change those thoughts with much more practical thoughts.

But here is what is different into mindfulness. When the inescapable pain of living rears its ugly head, we don't resist as well as struggle with it. We're currently fulfilling the soreness with kindness, gentleness, aware attention and a large dose of compassion. In a manner, both of us are actually drawing a series in the sand by handing over the car of needless fight and making significant life choices. We are just reluctant to allow our mental discomfort to stand between us and the place we would like to go. It has provided us much more time and effort to concentrate on doing what truly matters; living the lives of ours in tactics that resonate with our cores and as we do much more of, we have noticed that we are inclined to believe and feel good also. We are not saying any of this's simple. It will take commitment and practice.

Though the payoff may be profoundly life-altering. Our lives have been enriched in a lot of ways since we have discovered how to place the energies of ours to use for what is good. We are much less caught up in our uncomfortable heads & hearts and much more interested in doing what we are concerned about. We have seen this working with individuals who have sought our help including a huge number of individuals who have used our book. Our purpose is perfect for you to come up with the best value of your one life that is precious. Everything that we understand, we have crammed into this particular workbook that will help you on the way. These days it is the turn of yours.

This particular guide is actually meant to enable you to get something completely different by doing different things. Looking over this book - and internalizing everything you discover - is just one part of this process. But there is no guide on the environment, no tablet, no individual that may help make you live the life of yours in a particular way. You will decide to place what you discover into action. You're the only individual that is able to make the changes you have to make. In conclusion, you manage the path you want the life of yours to consider - that is the choice of yours.

There's a Buddhist stating that the journey of 1000 miles takes place with one step. Getting the hands of yours on this book is actually a step on a brand new path. Looking over this book, also up to this particular point, is still another step on the journey of yours out of the anxiety and into a new life.

A life lived nicely is the result of the selection of small moments. It will take a lifetime to produce life. Living based on your values is one thing we are going to help you do much more of, one stage at the same time. On the journey of yours, you will develop, progress and find out life in a way that you might certainly not have encountered before. The essential thing is, you are taking steps for minor actions that will ultimately take up you upwards a mountain. We invite you to come up with this book the travel guide of yours. Make use of the info here to make it easier to determine exactly where you wish to go. As you dedicate putting the values of yours into motion, the quality of the life of yours and of people around you will start improving.

Chapter 5: Mindfulness Methods And Mindfulness Meditation

"Joshua 1:8; This book of the law shall not depart out of thy mouth; but thou shalt meditate therein day and night, that thou mayest observe to do according to all that is written therein: for then thou shalt make thy way prosperous, and then thou shalt have good success."

• Mindfulness implores and utilizes distinctive path for its exercises. Being focused, exhaustive fixation, listening cautiously and completely conscious are the objectives of mindfulness strategies. It enables the mind to refocus on the present moments. All mindfulness systems are for the

most part types of meditation.
23

1. Fundamental mindfulness meditation – Sit unobtrusively and center around your normal breath or on a word or

"mantra" that you essentially repeat mutely. Give space for thoughts to travel immediately, subsequently profit to your thoughts for breath or mantra.

2. Body sensations – Notice unobtrusive body sensations like a tingle or shivering without judg

ment and allow them to pass. Notice each part of your body in progression from head to toe.

3. Sensory– Notice sights, sounds, smells, tastes, and touch. Name them "sights," "sound," "smell," "taste," or "touch" without judgment and allow them to go.

4. Feelings – enable feelings to be available without judgment. Watch a delicate and loos

ened up naming of feelings: "satisfaction," "outrage," "disappointment." acknowledge the presence of the feelings

without judgment and let them go.
5. Urge surfing –

address desires (for addictive substances or practices) and grant them to pass. Notice how your body feels as the longing enters. Substitute the desire for the longings to leave with the definite knowledge that it'll die down.

Mindfulness Meditation And different practices

Mindfulness will be acquired through mindfulness meditation, a methodical system of concentrating. You can figure out how to meditate over your own, after directions in books or tapes. Notwithstanding, you will appreciate the help of a teacher or group to answer questions and help you keep motivated. Search for someone utilizing meditation in a manner that goes along with your convictions and objectives.

On the off chance that you have an ailment, you will like a therapeutically balanced program that incorporates meditation. Ask your physician or hospital in regards to neighborhood gatherings. Insurance firms consistently covers the expense of meditation guidance.

Mindfulness meditation expands upon concentration practices. Here is the manner by which it works:

1. Go with the flow. In mindfulness meditation,

when you distinguish your concentration, you watch the progression of inward considerations, feelings, and real sensations without making a judgment about them as good or bad.

2. Focus.

You moreover might see external sensations like sounds, sights, and touch that make up your moment-to-moment experience. It isn't tied in with adhering to a particular arrangement, feelings or attempt to think back about the past. Rather, you watch what comes and go in your mind and discover that psychological propensities produce a feeling of well-being or enduring.

3. Remain with it.
Right now, this methods probably won't yield a better outcome however with time it will deliver achievement and expand it. Mindfulness practice includes tolerating regardless of what emerges in your conscious state right now. It includes being benevolent and forgiving toward yourself.

A few hints to stay in mind:

1. Gently divert. On the off chance that your mind meanders into planning, wandering off in fantasy land, or analysis, see any place it's gone and delicately send it to sensations in the present.

2. Try and try once more. On the off chance that you miss your expected meditation session, simply start again.

3. By working on tolerating your experience during meditation, it winds up simpler to effortlessly acknowledge whatever comes your way all through the rest of your day.

Mindfulness Exercises

On the off chance that mindfulness meditation appeals to you, progressing to a class or focusing on a meditation tape is a good method to begin. Meanwhile, here are some mindfulness practices you'll have the option to try on your own. These 5 exercises are some great approaches to begin.

1. Do a Mindful Body Scan

This basic exercise is an incredible method to get yourself feeling mindful and connect with your body. Doing this toward the beginning of the day can likewise assist you with getting your day away from work to a good start.

While sitting or resting on your bed (simply make a point not to sleep off on the off chance that you attempt this lying down!), take a couple of profound, mindful breaths. Notice the manner in which your breath enters and leaves your lungs.

Beginning with your toes, concentrate on each part of your body in turn.

Focus on how that zone is feeling and notice any impressions that you are encountering (Scott, n.d.). After a couple of seconds of centered consideration, move up to the next part of your body (i.e., after your toes, center around your feet, at that point lower legs, at that point calves, and so forth.).

This isn't just a good technique for placing you in a mindful state immediately, it can likewise enable you to see when your body is feeling differently in contrast to normal. You may get ailments or sickness that you wouldn't regularly see, just by taking a couple of moments every morning to scan your body.

You can get familiar with the mindful body scan and different activities here.
2.Write In A Journal/"Morning Pages"

Another great exercise that can assist you with setting the right mindful tone for the day is to write in your journal. A particular adaptation of this activity that is endorsed by author Julia Cameron is called "Morning Pages."

Here's the manner by which to utilize your diary as a stepping block to an increasingly mindful day.

Early in the morning, before you've taken off to work or school or began marking things off your long plan for the day, take a couple of moments to haul out your diary or a scratch pad and make an entry.

You can do another page every day and basically write how much you want to write, or you can attempt Cameron's Morning Pages work out:

"Morning Pages are three pages of longhand, continuous flow writing, accomplished before anything else. There is no incorrect method to do Morning Pages; they are not high workmanship. They are not even, "writing." They are tied in with everything without exception that enters your thoughts—and they are for your eyes as it were. Morning Pages incite, explain, comfort, persuade, organize, and synchronize the current day" (Cameron, n.d., as refered to in Scott, n.d.). Regardless of whether you follow Cameron's rules or not, taking only a couple of moments to record any mindless "chatter" in your mind or log any savvy dreams can clear your head and assist you with beginning your day off in a mindful state.

3. Envision Your Daily Goals

Envisioning your objectives is an astounding strategy for not just making it more probable that you will finish on your objectives, it can likewise assist you with ending up progressively mindful all the time.

At the point when you have define your every day objectives, take a couple of seconds to envision every one (Scott, n.d.).

See yourself undertaking every objective and finishing every objective today. Get as much detail as you can in your representation, so it feels genuine and inside your range.

At the point when you can see yourself checking that day by day objective off your list, proceed onward to the following objective and rehash until you have visualized the major aspect of your day to day objectives.

Practicing visualization of goal finishing can not just assist you with improving your focus and mindfulness, it can likewise bring down your pressure, improve your performance, upgrade your readiness, and give you the additional vitality or inspiration you may need to achieve everything on your list.

4. Go for a Mindful Nature Stroll
Exploiting the natural beauty around us is another great method to develop more prominent mindfulness.

Whenever you feel the requirement for a walk; regardless of whether it's a snappy excursion around the block or a lengthy walk through a spot; make it a careful nature walk.

It's quite easy to make any walk a mindful walk; you should simply connect every one of your faculties and remain mindful of what's going on both around you and inside you.

Be purposeful with your mindfulness; see your feet hitting the ground with each progression, see everything there is to see around you, open your ears to every one of the sounds encompassing you, feel each breathe in and breathe out, and just for the most part know about what's going on in every minute.

This activity encourages you connect with your legitimate self, however it additionally interfaces you to your condition and improves your consciousness of the magnificence that is all near, simply holding on to be found. Add these advantages to the known advantages of strolling consistently; brings down pressure, better heart wellbeing, and improves disposition—and you have one convenient exercise!

5. Conduct A Mindful Review Of Your Day

It very well may be anything but difficult to get drained and exhausted before

the day's over and let things slip. To assist you with keeping that mindful tone toward the day's end, attempt this activity.

Towards the end of your day, maybe after you finish the majority of your "must-dos" for the day or just before taking off to bed, take a couple of moments to do a survey of your day (Scott, n.d.).

Recall the beginning of the day and recollect your mindful practice that kicked everything off. Consider how it affected you.

Thoroughly consider the remainder of your day, being certain to take note of any particularly mindful moments or paramount occasions. Consider your disposition as you traveled through your every day schedule.

On the off chance that you need to monitor your advancement towards more prominent care, it's an extraordinary thought to record the majority of this in a diary or a journal; in any case, the fact of the matter is to offer yourself one more chance to be careful and end your day on the correct note.

Fundamental mindfulness meditation

This activity shows fundamental mindfulness meditation.

1. Sit on a straight-backed seat or with folded legs on the ground. Focus on a side of your breath, similar to the feelings of air gushing into your noses and out of your mouth, or your belly increasing and decreasing as you breathe in and inhale out.

2. When you've narrowed your concentration as such, begin to widen your interest. Become aware of sounds, sensations, and your ideas.

3. Grasp and consider each idea or sensation without making a judgment about it being positive or negative. On the off chance that your mind begins to race,

return your concentration to your presence. At that point extend your mindfulness again.

Figuring out how to stay in the present. A less proper way to deal with mindfulness can likewise help you to stay in the present and assume responsibility for your life. You can choose to practice mindfulness anytime you desire as it suits what you are doing. Utilizing these points can help:

1. Firstly, guide all focus to the feelings in your body
2. Breathe in through your nose, allowing the air descending into your lower abdomen. Give your abdomen a chance to extend completely.
3. Presently, slowly inhale through your mouth
4. Notice the sensation of each inward breath and exhalation

5. Continue with the job that needs to be done gradually and with full engagement
6. Draw in your senses completely. Notice

each sight, touch, and sound so you enjoy every sensation.

7. At the point when you see that your mind has meandered from the job needing to be done, delicately take your consideration back to the impressions existing apart from everything else.

Chapter 6: Breathing Exercises Technique

Any vocalist worth their salt will value the advantages of good breath control. Building up these aptitudes enhances a vocalist's capacity to sing louder, gentler, higher, lower, with controlled tone, with more power, hold notes or expressions for more, with controlled element and expression, and in addition augmenting the wellbeing of their vocal ropes. All the fun stuff basically. Breath control is one of, if not, THE most crucial method to ace for any vocalist. Whether you are a ultra-novice, or an accomplished vocalist, you have to have a work out for your breathing muscles frequently to make strides. Great breath control originates from "wellness" of the muscles, which should be frequently practiced to be kept up.

Anyway, on the off chance that it is so awesome, why don't we all practice our breathing constantly? Alternately why are the activities we are doing not living up to expectations? These are inquiries I have regularly asked, in connection to myself and in addition my understudies. These are some conceivable answers:-

It is exhausting It's diligent work Some understudies get to be disappointed with moderate advancement Practicing inaccurately can grow unfortunate propensities Students think that it hard to discover time inside of an occupied way of life Students may think that it hard to diagram advance naturally and hence lose inspiration to do it Some understudies don't realize what to do or how to function their breathing muscles without a mentor Many understudies do not have the protection or space to practice Some understudies regularly think that it more humiliating than honing other musical abilities like playing scales on a piano for instance Some understudies may not completely welcome the advantage to singing Some understudies think that it hard to apply breathing strategies to singing tunes The propensity for some singing understudies is to practice tunes, not singing procedures.

Sort (I) not knowing how to do it. In the event that you are not certain how to inhale accurately or how to hone your system, the best strategy is to have some individual vocal instructing. On the off chance that you are now having educational cost, approach your coach to recap this for you, and give you particular guidelines of what to rehearse. Attempt this activity to get to diaphragmatic relaxing. Lie on the floor with your knees up, and feet level on the floor. Keep up the common bend of your spine, so don't squash the little of your once more into the floor. In this position, take several casual moderate full breaths. Breathe in and breathe out completely every time. Presently put a book on your lower stomach area. As you breathe in you ought to see the book rise, and as you breathe out it will lower. This is diaphragmatic relaxing. On the off chance that the book is not going up when you breathe in, you are just filling the top piece of your lungs when you relax. Focus on moving the book up as you breathe in. When you have got the hang of this, attempt to rehash this movement in a standing position, and control you breathe in by taking in for four excludes then for four checks. Build up your control by expanding the quantity of numbers. Verify you keep up complete concentrate all through to guarantee your breathing muscles are moving effectively.

In what manner would we be able to handle the second sort of hindrance - not being propelled to isn't that right?

Chapter 7: Tips For Success

There are several ways to practice mindfulness but, however, you do it, your ultimate goal must be to alertness, focus and relaxation by way of deliberately and mindfully being aware of your thoughts, feelings, and emotions without any judgment. All forms of mindfulness are forms of meditation.

Basic Mindfulness – sit in peace, be quiet and concentrate on your breathing, or on a mantra or word that repeat to yourself silently. Allow your thoughts to enter and exit your mind without judging them.

Body Sensations – notice sensations in your body, such as an itch, and let them pass without judging them. Be aware of every part of your body from the top of your head to the tips of your toes.

Sensory – Notice all the sounds and the sights, the tastes the smells and touches.

Name each one and let it go, let it pass without judgment

Emotions – Allow your emotions to be there without judging them. Practice relaxed and steady naming of each emotion, accept that they are there and let them pass

Urge Surfing – Learn to cope with cravings, either for addictive behaviors or addictive substances. Focus on how your body feels as the craving begins and replace your wish that the craving would go with the certainty that it will go

Getting Started

Some forms of meditation involve concentration as their primary focus, either repeating a phrase over and over again or focusing on your breathing, allowing the thoughts that go through your mind to come and go without judgment. Concentrating mindfulness includes techniques like Tai Chi or Yoga and these can help to induce relaxation in your mind and body, allowing your stress levels to reduce. We know that mindfulness meditation builds on practicing concentration and here is how it works:

Go with the flow – as soon as you have established concentration, with mindfulness meditation you will observe your innermost emotions and thoughts, your body sensations and you will learn to let them pass without judging them, without labeling them as good or bad

Pay total attention – You will also begin to notice things that are going on around you – sights and sounds, touches that all live in your experience of life, moment to moment, things that you rarely ever notice. The real challenge here is not to get caught up on one specific sight, sound or touch – it is to watch everything equally, discover exactly which mental habits make you feel good and which ones make you feel bad

Keep it up – You may find, on occasion, that you don't feel relaxed at all, especially when you are just starting to learn. It is important that you keep it up, that you stay with it because, as time passes, you will begin to notice that you are happier that you are more self-aware and that are comfortable with a far wider range of experiences.

Practice Acceptance

The most important thing is that mindful practice leads to your acceptance of whatever comes along; whatever arises at each moment. It means that you must not be judgmental about yourself and you must be more forgiving towards yourself.

Redirect – if you find that your mind is wandering into daydreaming, criticism or planning, while you are practicing mindfulness, take note of where your mind has gone and learn how to redirect it, gently, back to the present

Keep trying – never give up. If you miss a session, just start over again. If you think it isn't working, it is, just keep on trying and do not give up. Even if it doesn't appear to be doing any good, it is.

If you can learn to accept the experience you have during meditation, you will find it much easier to accept anything that comes your way throughout the day.

Starting your mindfulness meditation journey can be easier if you attend a class or start out listening to CDs. Try this exercise on your own as well to learn the basic technique of mindfulness meditation

Sit cross-legged on the floor or on a chair that is straight-backed.

Focus on one aspect of your breath – perhaps how it feels when the air flows into your nose or out of your mouth. Perhaps on the sensation of your belly rising as you inhale and falling as you exhale

When you have learned to narrow down your concentration to just one part, start to widen out your focus Become more aware of sensations, sounds and the ideas that are flowing through your head

Embrace every thought, every sensation without judging it, without labeling it as bad or good. If your mind begins to wander or race, pull your focus right back to your breathing. Then start to expand your awareness once more.

Chapter 8: Shifting Out Of Negative Space

Many would think and imagine that clearing thoughts in your head through meditation naturally, means to eradicate all negative thoughts inside your head. No, it isn't. Whatever happened in your life experiences, it has been said and done and will always be a part of you serving as a contrast to let you know that it is a lesson learned and we close that chapter and move on. We still learn how to accept and honor ourselves completely in spite of those past negative experiences we may have. Meditating does not mean that you extract that part of your memory and forget all that has ever happened before.

Especially with life events that haven't served you well, more than anything in this world you would like the "pain and suffering" to be taken away. But you must know, that our mind is like the revolving earth, ever evolving and spinning in its orbit in its own perfect proximity and what-ever that's been planted before, it is there, and always will be. Because it is so wide and limitless, we can choose where we would like to lead our thoughts. Our mind is the limitless space, and "negative" spaces are fundamental to building an "image and picture" of anything we wish to put together. That is how we are able to visualize dreams, scenarios, circumstances and fragments of things we have come to learn and know about. We put those pieces together inside our heads.

When you learn to "unclutter" the mind, you get to choose to be on the other side of the "negative space" that is part of your brain and living mind and you can't turn that part "off" like a switch. You can only ever attempt to make the effort for a "shift" into a different space. When you "quiet" the mind, you see more clearly and there is a small window of opportunity to make the "shift" when that happens. Slowly, steadily, you shift yourself to a different space---a positive one. One that contains new affirmations and thoughts, new memories, experiences, and places you have recreated for yourself.

Planting new seeds takes time for it to grow and also takes consistent care for it to ensure that it is healthy and strong before you can bear fruits and flowers for you to enjoy and repeat the cycle. It is a process, a journey, a learning curve for the mind to adjust and know its way around. Just like anybody you first come to know as a stranger, our minds are the same and it could be our potential best friend or worst enemy. You can make the effort to understand her strengths and weaknesses to make the "relationship" work or you can resist, resent it, and feel like it is a battle and challenge every day, and feel the need to fight against it all day long. It is a choice we all have and we can make it work to our advantage.

Meditation doesn't necessarily mean sitting in a chair or on a floor and just closing your eyes in a dead quiet room that could echo your breath and forcing your mind to stop the chatter. In the beginning, this would probably be counteractive to your first step of taking the leap to have control of your mind. It would probably work better if you used other tools or routines to help jumpstart your mind, and introduce new positive things and subjects into it before you begin to sift and sort through your clutter. Yoga is one of the methods that best serves as a physical and also a mental workout, producing best results for both body and mind.

Because you literally hold your own physical body as your object of attention, all the focus and concentration put on it will ultimately produce positive results if you commit wholeheartedly and go into the postures with intent and give it your undivided attention. If you do it consciously for a full 60 – 90 minutes every day, that would definitely lead you feeling a whole lot better releasing all kinds of tensions and stress in your body and mind with your attention taken away from any feelings of negativity in that frame of time and put right onto your physical body directly to tone and strengthen. It is by far one of the most effective practices for easily distracted individuals.

You can of course pick up a quieter and more subtle routine and habit like a good self-development read, (if exercising is a big issue for you for whatever reason) books of a positive nature and feed your mind with more "good stuff" so that you can "fill it up" with new knowledge that is applicable in your daily activities and one that serves you well. Painting nature also serves as an extremely good way to put your attention on bright colors and natural feel-good settings and environment over a good period of an hour straight, uninterrupted with your mind stationed in a good, happy place. It is a little obscure as people always have this idea that only professional artists can pick up that paintbrush to do something like that.

But really, you don't need to be Picasso to attempt to engage in this activity. If you have a love for nature, it will not be a difficult task for you to set your eyes on it for a full hour, however, your painting turn out to become is totally irrelevant and only serves as an outlet to grab hold of your attention. The more positive activities and attitudes you choose to include into your daily life activities, the easier the road to be able to sit down and literally do nothing and naturally be able to quiet you mind come quickly.

You will no longer have to use external tools to aid you in doing so. It will just be you, your space, and your mind. That is the ultimate goal eventually. Not having to meditate while you're in an awkward pose (yoga) or having to set your eyes on something beautiful to do so (on nature) will be the best outlet to go about because you take yourself, and your mind, everywhere you go.

You can't always carry your yoga mat with you 24/7, or readily have paints and brushes in your bag pack, or a new book constantly at the back of your palms. So if you can eventually do it with nothing in your hands, or on your plate to "keep you occupied", you will have successfully achieved the best method to do your meditation. To simply just sit there, close your eyes and let it all go. To allow well-being to enter with ease and flow, making the shift to the positive space of everything you ever desired for and want in your life.

Chapter 9: Four Noble Truths

The journey of mindfulness through the teachings of Buddha and Dharma include the recognition of the four noble truths. These four noble truths are the four central beliefs that contain the essence of the entire Buddhist teachings. You will now learn what these four noble truths are, and how they directly relate to your journey to mindfulness. Remember, this journey and these truths are open to anyone who desires to lead a more mindful and peaceful existence. You are not required to be a part of any specific religion or to be a monk to learn about and grow from these beliefs. They are simply teachings that are open to anyone who desires to take the inner journey to mindfulness.

Noble Truth #1: Suffering Exists

The Buddhist view is that all life consists of varying levels of suffering and dissatisfaction. As you have already learned, this type of suffering is called Dukkha.

The very nature of humanity is imperfect, and so is the world in which you live. Throughout your entire lifetime, you will inevitably endure various degrees of physical suffering. This includes pain, injury, sickness, old age, tiredness, and eventually death. This type of suffering is especially true for people who are poor.

Knowing this, you can realize that you are never able to permanently keep all that you strive for, and that eventually, everything will pass you by. Happiness will pass you by, and eventually, you yourself will pass by, too.

Noble Truth #2: Suffering Arises from Attachment to Desires

We all inevitably suffer, just as we all inevitably have desires. The specific desires that are considered in this teaching are those relating to the desire to control things, such as cravings and sensual pleasures. This type of suffering is called "samudaya" or "tanha". An example of this type of suffering is if you desire for fame and fortune. As a result of your desires, you are destined to experience the suffering that comes with disappointment and in that path, you may even cause suffering to others around you.

When you attach yourself or your emotions to material things, you create suffering within' yourself because attachments don't last, and due to the law of impermanence, loss is inevitable. As a result of these experiences, attachment to desires leads to the necessary following of suffering.

Noble Truth #3: Suffering Ceases when Attachment to Desire Ceases

Naturally, if you are able to cease your attachment to material things, then you cease the suffering that comes with that attachment. The ending of suffering in this way is called "nirodha". This means that you have successfully achieved Nirvana, which is the state you enter when you finally liberate yourself from suffering. When you enter Nirvana, your mind experiences complete liberation, freedom, and non-attachment. In this state, you are able to let go of any desire or craving. Nirvana is the process of attaining the state of dispassion.

When you achieve Nirvana, you achieve a state where you are free from all worries, all troubles, and all ideas. As much as you may try, it is impossible to comprehend this state unless you, yourself, achieve it.

Noble Truth #4: Freedom from Suffering is Possible by Practicing the Eightfold Path

The path to end suffering is known as the "Eightfold Path". This path allows you to attain liberation from suffering and is often what is referred to as "enlightenment" by many people.

The path that enables you to end suffering in your life is gradual and occurs as you continue on the journey of self-improvement through eight elements. Believe it or not, the Eightfold Path can actually extend over many lifetimes, throughout which you experience is subject every individual rebirth

to karmic conditioning. Through each lifetime you will notice that the sufferings associated with cravings, ignorance, and other effects will gradually disappear. When they have completely disappeared, then you have achieved the state of Nirvana.

The Eightfold Path

As you realize that the Eightfold Path is the path to liberation from suffering, you may wish to learn more about what this path is. This path is one that you must take if you desire to totally free yourself from suffering. The following eight attitudes or paths are the "right" or correct things that you must do in life:

1.RightView
 2.RightIntention
 3.RightSpeech
 4.RightAction
 5.RightLivelihood

6. RightEffort
7. RightMindfulness
8. Right Concentration

When you achieve this "right" way of life, you can successfully achieve Nirvana. As you can see, mindfulness itself is one of the noble truths, and as you read this book you will learn exactly how you can achieve the Right Mindfulness along your journey.

As you read about the Buddhist terms of suffering, you should realize that it is not the same as the English definition of suffering. In English, suffering implies that a person is in dire need of something in order to survive. In Buddhist teachings, suffering implies that we are all in a constant state of suffering, which we are not.

In understanding the four noble truths and the marks of existence, you can come to realize some profound things about your success in life. Due to the inevitable existence of impermanence, you can assure that you will never be living in the same situation for too long. For some period of time, you may find that you are struggling deeply and that it feels as though hard times are persistent. However, knowing the law of impermanence means that you can feel confident that very soon you will be enduring good times once again. Likewise, you must realize that good times are also impermanent and life can turn around in an instant and the troublesome times will arise once again.

It is best for your success if you do not remain attached to specific outcomes or situations. You should not become attached to actually achieving success, because then when it disappears inevitably, you will suffer more than you may have if you recognized that it would soon be gone. Still, knowing that success will come and go just like the bad times will come and go, it doesn't mean you should not maintain goals in your life. Having a positive purpose and working towards positive goals allows you to have a more peaceful and happy life overall, which is important. Those who do not have goals to work towards will end up having more hard times than positive, which leads to a lack of balance and a lack of internal peace.

"We are shaped by our thoughts; we become what we think. When the mind is pure, joy follows like a shadow that never leaves".

- Buddha

As Buddha himself says, you need to recognize the importance of your thoughts, and therefore keeping them positive and maintaining your mindfulness no matter what situation you are in. Doing so will allow you to carry a mind that is pure, and therefore you will be able to lead a life filled with joy and happiness. It is important that you always maintain a clear awareness of your thoughts and stay mindful of what you allow to come in and how you allow it to affect you. As a result, you will be able to lead a life rich with inner peace.

Chapter Summary:

- There are four noble truths in life
- They are: suffering exists, suffering arises from attachment to desires, suffering ceases when attachment to desires ceases, freedom from suffering is possible by the eightfold path
- The eightfold path includes eight "rules" of life that can assist you in reaching nirvana
- You should still maintain a positive mind despite being in hard times and knowing hard times will come back.
- We become what we think

Chapter 10: Meditation For Better Sleep

Sleep is one of the ways to make you healthy and fit. When you rest well, you have the capacity to have a good day ahead of you. Waking up when you are fresh is the first step to a good day. Let us look at the various meditation techniques that will aid you enjoy better sleep.

Guided meditation for sleep is a way to help you let go of any worrying thoughts and relax the body before you can sleep. Just like other forms of meditation that you have come across, you need to move the focus from the mind to the sensations in the body. When you practice this meditation regularly, you tend to sleep better, meaning that you can handle the issues that come with sleeping.

Research by the American Sleep Association shows that more than 30 percent of the adults have problems with falling asleep or maintaining sleep. Research also shows that more than 30 percent of the adults will get less than 7 hours of sleep each night.

When you sleep better, you will be able to improve your immunity, and you will function at your best. If you have a problem with anxiety, you will be able to handle it better if you meditate before you sleep.

The aim of guided sleep meditation is to reduce the effect of worries and tension that build up in your body before you can sleep. When you learn to focus and then relax the body, you will notice massive improvements in the ability to sleep.

Benefits

Guided meditation for sleep allows you to move out of the past and the future and focus on the present. Usually, when you lie down to sleep, you usually swim in thoughts that were suppressed in the daytime. Without any help, controlling emotions can be hard.

When you use guided sleep meditation, you get to let go of the thoughts that are going through your head. When you relax, the heart rate goes down, and the breathing rate also slows. All of these make you ready to sleep better. Many of the guided sleep meditation exercises will have you follow an audio guide that you can use on the radio or through your phone. You get guided via the voice in the audio. With time, you get to follow the prompts in the audio, and you ding that you calm down when meditating.

The Process: You first have to get an audio recording of the meditation. You can look it up in various stored online or go for a free recording. You need to lie down comfortably and play the audio. This way, you get to redirect the attention away from your thoughts to your body using what is called a body scan. This process means you let go of your thoughts and then focus on the sensations in the body without the need to change them. Try and move through the different parts of the body, starting from the head to the toes. Make sure you notice the different sensations that you feel when moving through the feelings. The audio will tell you which part to go through and what sensations to look out for. Apart from the body scan, you can go for the breathing exercise, visualization, and gratitude as some form of meditation.

Chapter 11: Thought Awareness

Thought awareness is one of the most important aspects of being mindful. Most people never get a chance to think about their thoughts. The ability to examine your own thoughts can be empowering. You can choose to avoid dwelling on certain types of thoughts. You can also keep focusing on the thoughts that have a positive impact in your mind.

You can do a thought awareness exercise with the breathing exercise discussed in chapter one. When you are doing your breathing exercise, you will often be distracted by the thoughts that pass through your mind. You will be tempted to entertain these thoughts. Some of them are important and positive while others are just distractions and may even have a negative impact in your life.

There are no bad and good thoughts

We often classify thoughts as either positive of negative. We try to entertain positive thoughts while we try to ignore negative ones. However, our classification system for our thoughts is subjective.

When trying to achieve mindfulness, you should avoid judging thoughts. Instead, you should just observe them from a third person point of view. They exist independently from you. You always have the choice either to entertain these thoughts or to let them be.

You should coexist with your thoughts

When doing your mindfulness exercises, you should avoid dwelling on your thoughts with prejudice. You should keep your mind focused on the task. However, you should not completely ignore the thoughts. Instead, acknowledge that they exist. Meditation masters compare this experience to a boulder in a stream. You should imagine yourself as a giant boulder in a slow moving stream. The water around you should not be able to move you or erode your parts. Your thoughts are like the water and the debris around the rock. They are temporary.

Keep important thoughts

Your fleeting thoughts come and go fast. If your mind is in a hyperactive state, you may miss and forget some important thought. To avoid this from happening, you should keep a notepad with you at all times. In your thought awareness sessions, you should let most of your unimportant thoughts pass by while you should take down the ones that you may need in the future.

By being aware of all the flow of your thoughts, you will be able to learn how to separate your behavior from your thoughts. Most people who are under extreme stress become a victim of the flow of their thoughts. Their behavior is affected by the high amount of thoughts flowing in their minds. People who never learn to be mindful do not know how to deal with this when it happens.

By keeping track of the flow of your thoughts, you will be able to know if you are under stress. You will be able to adjust exposure to your sources of stress before your physical and mental health is affected. You will be better suited to cope with your common sources of stress.

Chapter 12: Ways To Be Mindful At Work

Add chapterWork is a very important part of our lives. Many of us get caught up in doing things for other people, and not prioritizing correctly. So what is the cost of not being mindful? Not being aware and meditative? You guessed it – it's your life, man – your whole life!

So I'm going to suggest to you some pretty trusted and self-implemented ideas which I have used in my working time. They are amazingly awesome. This is called "regular mindful check-ins". Check-ins are great for keeping you on track. What you have to do is:

Mindful Bells. Put on an alarm – at whatever intervals you think you need, have a melodious alarm go off that everybody can hear. The role of the alarm is to remind yourself/or your staff to be mindful, more loving. You can use visual mindfulness reminders – and it has worked wonders for me. Put up photos of things you love – your pet, your wife, your children – whatever it is. Have their photos in front of you and use these as reminders. You can even put up pictures of ocean scenes, nature – whatever it is that soothes your mind. if you put up these pictures, the effect is amazing. If you are truly serious about your life I would recommend it; I will fold my hands and beg you to please do this step – it is amazing.

How You Do Mindful Check-Ins:

Start taking a deep, slow, conscious breath. Physically stop where you are, and take a seat for a moment.

Take the awareness into your physical body and notice how it feels – is there any tension in the body? Notice any feelings of energy or tiredness, relaxation or aches; notice the touch of clothing on skin, and any other sensations like temperature, pressure – aiming to feel what is there without any judgment.

Tune into you emotional and mental states. Notice any kinds of thoughts in your mind. Check out the entire state of mind calmly and with focus, and examine any emotions that are present.

Open your awareness to take the whole entire present moment in - the sound of the day, how you are feeling, what your perceptions are in your mind – open up the present moment.

Proceed with awareness.

Meditate Regularly:

I cannot emphasize this enough. I am not sure which meditation processes you would like to proceed with, but there are many! I would really recommend that you question yourself and understand who you are, and then only proceed with meditation. There is great confusion in what meditation practices there are – very few will understand who you are. And I'm sure that you will pick the right one – go ahead, believe in yourself, and do meditation in the morning and the evening for five minutes – whatever it is. If you feel like you need more meditation tips, leave a review for this book, and I will find them and I will share more amazing things. And do remember – I love you. And there are no hidden intentions .

Heres one more technique which cough my eye..

STOP.

S = Stop. Literally, stop. Whenever you feel heavy and whenever you are in a situation where you are not in the mood, or there is an emotion taking a toll on you, stop there.

T = Take a breather, buddy! You have to take a breath – long ones but slowly..

O = Observe. Now you again have to be present. This is similar to what we have discussed previously. Observe the emotion. Once you observe it, it will subside, and you can relax.

P = Proceed. When you understand what is happening, then ask yourself – what's the next move? And then proceed.

Chapter 13: Dealing With Distractions While Meditating

Despite having concerted efforts to maintain a state of mindfulness, the mind may wander. It may suddenly jump to past or anticipated experiences--a novel you read long ago, friends not seen for years, a future meeting, a trip on the coming weekend, etc. The moment you notice that your mind is no longer focused on your breath or body, consciously bring your mind back to meditation. Below are some suggestions to aid you maintain the concentration needed for the practice of mindfulness.

1. Counting

When you are distracted, counting may help. Its purpose is simply to refocus the mind on your breathing. Once your mind is refocused, give up counting. There are numerous ways to do this and they should all be done mentally. Some of the techniques are as follows:

a) While inhaling, count "one, one, one..." until fresh air fills your lungs. While exhaling, count "two, two, two..." until the fresh air empties your lungs. Then while inhaling again, count "three, three, three..." and "four, four, four..." upon exhalation. Count until ten and repeat until the mind is focused on the breath.

b) The second technique is counting quickly up to ten. Breathe in while counting "one, two, three, four,... nine and ten" and again breathe out while counting "one, two, three, four,...nine and ten". Do this again as many times as necessary to focus the mind on the breath.

2. Connecting

Do not wait for the brief pause after exhaling but connect the exhaling and inhaling. This lets you notice both breaths as one continuous breath.

3. Fixing

After connecting your inhalation and exhalation, fix your focus on the point where you feel that your inhaling breath and exhaling breath touch one another. Notice your breaths moving in and out, rubbing, or touching the rims of your nostrils.

4. Focus the mind like a carpenter

When a carpenter wants to cut a board, he draws a line on it. Then by using his handsaw he cuts through the board along the drawn line. His focus is not on the teeth or the saw as they shift in and out of the board. Instead, his entire focus is placed on the line he has drawn so he could straightly cut the board. In a similar fashion, you should keep your focus straight on the spot where you experience your breath coming in contact with the rims of your nostrils.

5. Your mind acting as a gatekeeper

A gatekeeper would not notice the specific details of people. His attention may only be focused on the general movement or number of people going in and out of the house through the gate. Likewise, during mindfulness meditation, do not take into consideration any specific element of your experiences. You simply focus on the feeling of your inhalation and exhalation as they enter and leave the rims of your nostrils.

With continuous practice, you will have a light feeling in your mind and body. It feels so light that it seems you are springing towards the sky or floating on water. After your gross in-breaths and out-breaths abate, subtler breathing follows. When a sign-object appears for the first time, a subtler sign-object will replace it. You can compare this subtlety with the ringing of a bell.

When someone strikes the bell with a huge iron rod, there is a gross sound heard at first. Eventually, the sound fades and becomes extremely soft. Just as with your practice, the first few in-and-out breathings appear as a gross sign. With more and more attention placed to breathing, the sign becomes so subtle. Meanwhile your consciousness stays completely paying attention on the rims of your nostrils.

As the sign develops, more objects of meditation become clearer and the breath becomes subtler. It will become so subtle that you will not anymore notice the existence of your breaths. At this point, do not be disappointed thinking nothing is happening to your practice because you lost your breath. Do not worry and just be determined and mindful enough to bring back the sensation of breathing at rims of your nostrils. This is the time you must perform more vigorous practice, balancing your mindfulness, self-trust, patience, determination and wisdom.

Chapter 14: Mindfulness Can Improve Your Relationships

Possibly you are seeking a way to approach life with steadier outlook, a more positive mentality, and a healthier way of handing your interactions with others. You may be searching for better ways to manage challenging situations. Perhaps you understand that it is important to not only be physically fit, but also emotionally steady. Mindfulness can help you achieve these benefits, and in doing so can have a very positive impact on your personal relationships. Mindfulness is a powerful aid in managing and resolving conflicts. In addition, every benefit of mindfulness training is important for strengthening your ability to navigate your own personal relationships in positive ways.

What are the benefits of mindfulness in your personal life?

Practicing mindfulness techniques requires you to become more familiar with yourself. You listen to your body better, and as you meditate, you will begin to understand yourself, including your strengths and your weaknesses. You will become more aware of your actions and emotions, and whether you are interacting with others in positive or negative ways. As you become more aware of yourself, you will be able to take steps to increase the positive, and reduce or eliminate the negative emotions that you feel.

Mindfulness techniques are incredibly useful to help you develop the ability to manage your relationships effectively. When problems arise, you can recognize and deal with the problem. You will also be able to focus on the actual problem, releasing anger and negativity that are like poisons in relationships.

You can learn to observe and acknowledge your thoughts, feelings, and emotions without allowing them to spiral out of control. Mindfulness meditation enables you to remain focused on the situation, instead of being completely distracted by your feelings about the situation. Achieving this takes training, but mastering mindfulness techniques will enable you to remain in a calmer, more confident state of mind.

When you are in a relationship, being able to handle negative emotions, including anger, using mindfulness techniques, strengthens your relationship by giving attention to the positive, while controlling or eliminating the negative aspects. Not placing blame, behaving in anger, or feeling tense and unhappy paves the way for resolving any conflict or issues in a fair, positive manner that is good for you and good for your relationship.

Can mindfulness techniques be used to help you forgive others?

Mindfulness is a powerful tool that you can use to calm your mind, view situations in a more understanding and open-minded light, become more empathetic, and it can help you forgive others. You will be able to focus not only on the actions of others, but your own actions as well.

You can use mindfulness techniques to get rid of negative emotions that an event or situation has caused you. Recall the event, and concentrate on the person involved.

In order to forgive the person, you need to recall the anger you feel, but also deal with it and expel it in order to forgive.

Focus on the person and how angry you feel. Remove every other thought from your mind. Without actively participating in your emotions, think about how you feel when you look at that person's face.

Now you're going to forgive that person. Give yourself permission to let go of the anger, and allow yourself to forgive. Repeat to yourself that the person can no longer cause you negative emotions. You can no longer be hurt by this person.

Allow your anger to leave your body with each breath. Your eyes should remain closed, and you must fully concentrate on your breath as it travels from your nose to your lungs. Focus as your chest expands and then the breath is expelled from your lungs, along with your negative feelings of anger. Continue for as long as necessary. It can take time to truly forgive the person. When you are ready, open your eyes.

How are your relationships improved by mindfulness?

Specifically, mindfulness helps you to be your best self. You will feel more centered, serene, and in control of your emotions. Mastering mindfulness techniques can greatly improve your overall outlook, and all of these positive elements work in tandem to improve your relationships too.

As you read earlier, mindfulness meditation techniques strengthen your immune system, reducing stress, and eliminating negative energy. The way you react to everything and everybody around you is influenced by your new attitude, feelings, and behaviors.

What is the best way to use mindfulness to help your relationships?

Any change takes time and consistency. The best way to incorporate mindfulness into your life and to use it to improve your relationships is to establish a routine. As you practice mindfulness, you will see positive results. Your mindfulness results will increase over time, and your relationships will benefit. Remember, stick with it!

Chapter 15: Mindfulness Can Improve Your Relationships

Possibly you are seeking a way to approach life with steadier outlook, a more positive mentality, and a healthier way of handing your interactions with others. You may be searching for better ways to manage challenging situations. Perhaps you understand that it is important to not only be physically fit, but also emotionally steady. Mindfulness can help you achieve these benefits, and in doing so can have a very positive impact on your personal relationships. Mindfulness is a powerful aid in managing and resolving conflicts. In addition, every benefit of mindfulness training is important for strengthening your ability to navigate your own personal relationships in positive ways.

What are the benefits of mindfulness in your personal life?

Practicing mindfulness techniques requires you to become more familiar with yourself. You listen to your body better, and as you meditate, you will begin to understand yourself, including your strengths and your weaknesses. You will become more aware of your actions and emotions, and whether you are interacting with others in positive or negative ways. As you become more aware of yourself, you will be able to take steps to increase the positive, and reduce or eliminate the negative emotions that you feel.

Mindfulness techniques are incredibly useful to help you develop the ability to manage your relationships effectively. When problems arise, you can recognize and deal with the problem. You will also be able to focus on the actual problem, releasing anger and negativity that are like poisons in relationships.

You can learn to observe and acknowledge your thoughts, feelings, and emotions without allowing them to spiral out of control. Mindfulness meditation enables you to remain focused on the situation, instead of being completely distracted by your feelings about the situation. Achieving this takes training, but mastering mindfulness techniques will enable you to remain in a calmer, more confident state of mind.

When you are in a relationship, being able to handle negative emotions, including anger, using mindfulness techniques, strengthens your relationship by giving attention to the positive, while controlling or eliminating the negative aspects. Not placing blame, behaving in anger, or feeling tense and unhappy paves the way for resolving any conflict or issues in a fair, positive manner that is good for you and good for your relationship.

Can mindfulness techniques be used to help you forgive others?

Mindfulness is a powerful tool that you can use to calm your mind, view situations in a more understanding and open-minded light, become more empathetic, and it can help you forgive others. You will be able to focus not only on the actions of others, but your own actions as well.

You can use mindfulness techniques to get rid of negative emotions that an event or situation has caused you. Recall the event, and concentrate on the person involved. In order to forgive the person, you need to recall the anger you feel, but also deal with it and expel it in order to forgive.

Focus on the person and how angry you feel. Remove every other thought from your mind. Without actively participating in your emotions, think about how you feel when you look at that person's face.

Now you're going to forgive that person. Give yourself permission to let go of the anger, and allow yourself to forgive. Repeat to yourself that the person can no longer cause you negative emotions. You can no longer be hurt by this person.

Allow your anger to leave your body with each breath. Your eyes should remain closed, and you must fully concentrate on your breath as it travels from your nose to your lungs. Focus as your chest expands and then the breath is expelled from your lungs, along with your negative feelings of anger. Continue for as long as necessary. It can take time to truly forgive the person. When you are ready, open your eyes.

How are your relationships improved by mindfulness?

Specifically, mindfulness helps you to be your best self. You will feel more centered, serene, and in control of your emotions. Mastering mindfulness techniques can greatly improve your overall outlook, and all of these positive elements work in tandem to improve your relationships too.

As you read earlier, mindfulness meditation techniques strengthen your immune system, reducing stress, and eliminating negative energy. The way you react to everything and everybody around you is influenced by your new attitude, feelings, and behaviors.

What is the best way to use mindfulness to help your relationships?

Any change takes time and consistency. The best way to incorporate mindfulness into your life and to use it to improve your relationships is to establish a routine. As you practice mindfulness, you will see positive results. Your mindfulness results will increase over time, and your relationships will benefit. Remember, stick with it!

Chapter 16: Thoughts Are Not Facts

What you feel in your body is most of the times the result of what you have been thinking. You have what is called the "Monkey Mind". Sometimes the mind runs wild jumping from thought to thought. It can even mix thoughts about recent things with thoughts about things that happened decades ago, and it seems impossible to calm the mind. In any case, there's a misconception that when you meditate you are supposed to stop all thinking. Not quite like that!

There are two important things to know about meditation and thoughts.

First - Meditation is not about getting rid of your thoughts. It is about learning how to be at ease with them and how you acknowledge becoming distracted by them.

Second - Thoughts are not facts, and you are not your thoughts. You should not identify yourself with your thoughts, and just because you are thinking it doesn't mean it is happening or will ever happen.

It is really worth remembering that emotions come and go, thoughts come and go, and you can allow them to come and go, even if they seem to be stuck there for a whole day or a whole week. They do eventually change, and they move on more easily if you bring awareness to them. Not thinking about them, but just bringing gentle awareness to them. Acknowledging they are there without fighting them.

It is very important to know that the secret practice of mindfulness is compassion. If you can learn to not fight with yourself you might learn to be responsive, not reactive to stressful moments.

I really encourage you in your practice to really see if you can not fight with yourself. Come to some kind of diplomatic agreement, some sort of compromise. If you find yourself fighting, free yourself a bit. Stop the practice and relax a bit. Allow yourself to relax within the practice and then go back to it.

Learning to work with yourself is the way in which you might learn to work with others. For that, you need attitudes of patience, trust, and non-judgment. Being mindful doesn't mean being peaceful. Sometimes it means being very strong, clear, and prepared.

Exercise – Mindful Movements

In mindfulness you work with feelings so they cause you less harm. You can also do it in movement, when you are active. It can be done walking or practicing yoga, qigong, tai chi or other similar moves.

So now, you'll be practicing some yoga movements using mindfulness. Yoga is described by Patanjali, the yogi who wrote the Yoga Sutras, as: "Stopping the fluctuation of the mind to find the true Self." So if you want to really be with yourself without that mental chatter, you can use mindful movements.

You can do it even deeper by paying attention to your movements, on purpose, in the present moment, without judgement. Remember that when you are sensing, the brain interrupts the thinking process. So, every day, you can practice yoga and mindfulness to calm your mind and relax your body to protect yourself from the harmful consequences of stress.

So, as an example, you'll do just a few asanas (yoga poses) for you to see the difference between mindfulness in stillness and in movement.

Tadasana (Mountain Pose)

Stand up and start with Tadasana, the Mountain Pose.

Spread the feet hip-width apart. Lift and spread your toes wide, and press the floor with the balls of your feet. Explore what happens in the feet and calf muscles. Feel the contact with the ground, the temperature of your feet, the temperature and the texture of the ground.

Unlock your knees, engage your thighs and really feel what you are doing. Don't do it automatically. Really be aware of these movements and the sensations in your body.

Tuck your tailbone, make sure your spine is long and tall and realize the tiniest sensations in your spine while you do this.

Roll your shoulders up and back. The arms behind the line of the body with palms wide open. Really sense the palms opening.

Slightly tuck the chin to the chest and look in front or, if you want, close your eyes. Become aware of all your body from the bottom to the top. Feel that sense of standing tall and strong.

Uttanasana (Standing Forward Bend)

Inhale and, with full awareness, slowly raise your arms to the ceiling. Feel the muscles moving.

Palms facing forward and, with the spine and the arms very straight, as you exhale, very gently, bend from the waist, and bring the trunk and the arms down. Can you feel the air flying between the fingers on the way down? Really sense the palms opening and the air flying between the fingers. Really sense the whole body changing.

Sense the contact of the palms with the ground or maybe your shin bones or knees, if you can't touch the ground. Feel how this posture stretches your back and hamstrings.

Marjaryasana (Cat and Cow Movement)

Come to table top and sense the palms and knees in contact with the mat.

The knees must be aligned with the hips and the hands with the shoulders.

Inhale, drop the belly. Feel the belly going down. Feel the curvature in your spine. Raise the chest. Feel the abdomen expanding.

Exhale, suck the belly, round the upper back, and lower your head.

Keep doing these movements, bringing total awareness to every breath and every move in the body, feeling every vertebra, every muscle, even the little sensations.

Keep doing it at your own pace and you might discover how this movement changes the way you breath. See what happens with your breath as you move up and down.

Here you can decide if you want to stay safe or if you want to explore just how far you can go, by doing circular movements, and challenging yourself. Breathe in, drop the belly, move to the right and front. Breathe out, suck the belly, move to the left and back.

See what you like. Are you willing to push yourself beyond what is comfortable? Or do you want to stay very safe with flat and small movements?

Balasana (Child's Pose)

Bring your buttocks to your heels. Lower your torso over your upper legs and feel all of these points of contact.

Place your forehead on the ground and the arms rest on the floor beside the legs. Become still and just for a moment close the eyes and feel the body in stillness, noticing any sensations in the fingertips, legs, shoulders. Noticing the breath, the movements of the breath. Stay in this pose as long as is comfortable to you and then come up.

Mindful Movements Exercise Summary

Sequence: Tadasana / Uttanasana / Marjariasana / Balasana

Whichever asanas or sequence you perform, the idea is to focus on things, such as:

- Points of contact between the body and the mat

- Temperature of the body

- Movement of the muscles

- Pattern of the breath

- The air on your skin

- Tingling, numbness, and the tiniest sensations

Tips to Remember!

- Try to practice mindful movements every day as it will help you stay focused on sensations rather than thoughts.

- Don't judge what you are doing and how you are feeling. Just take the experience as it is.

- Acknowledge when you become distracted by the thoughts and come back to the senses.

- This is just a quick example of asanas you can perform to first try mindful movements. If you already practice yoga and have a sound knowledge of the asanas, please, feel free to choose your own sequence. Vinyasa yoga is particularly suitable for mindful movements as the flow of the sequence allows you to be more focused.

- If you don't practice yoga, try other sports like jogging or walking, or simply focus on your day-to-day movements.

 Self-Reflection

How was to do these asanas?

How was it to notice all of this?

What did you learn for yourself?

What differences do you feel of practicing mindfulness in movement and in stillness?

How would you describe the feelings and sensations in your body?

How do you feel mindfulness can help you when doing yoga or other sports?

Did you enjoy it?

The idea of this mindful movement practice is not necessarily about enjoyment, but many people do find it when they practice. They feel more whole, more calm, more connected with their body.

The main thing though is that you learn to bring awareness to your body and breath, feelings and thoughts as you're doing this practice.

When you're doing these movements might be that you learn something about yourself, but the main thing is that you can choose how far you want to go. I'd like you to be very aware of your choice. The way of reducing stress in life is to become aware, to become mindful of choice.

Chapter 17: Guide To Practicing The Meditation

Build up a sense of peaceful focus and relax into the posture that you have selected. A beginner might take some time to settle, however, once you have developed into your meditation posture; you may check up the 4 basics of mindfulness, these are officially called the four frames of positions that you may study. You may try them in tandem or simply one at a time.

You must become mindful of the body and the sensations you are feeling. However, do not stress yourself out by trying too hard. Let it flow. You will naturally slip in and out of mindfulness, especially as a beginner. If you're unsure about what to focus on, try body-mindfulness, which can be thought of as focusing, mentally noting and exploring the component parts of the body like the hair, head, muscles, stomach, teeth, skin, heart, bones, etc. The practice is to focus on where they are, what they do, what they are reliant on, and so on.

*Focus on every part of your body and observe it. You may discover that the thing itself becomes clearer in some way or takes place as a mental image.

*Focusing on "breathing in and breathing out" is even known as mindfulness. In fact, the base of all meditation and mindfulness is to focus on the breath.

*Movement and the way it interacts and reacts with events is one more aspect to study. Muscle tension, tiredness and other experiences. The body fights against plenty of physical experiences, but it is simply an inactive and senseless piece of meat, bones, and skin if the mind is not working in harmony with it.

*Additional characteristics to study are physical characteristics, such as the temperature of your body, for example.

Inspect the 2nd foundation, mindfulness of sensations and physical feelings. To make a distinction from the body-mindfulness, this foundation of mindfulness is often referred to as body-states meditation.

When and how sensations occur in a human body is considered to be one of the things that we need to be focused on. What caused this sensation? Are they neutral, pleasant, or unpleasant? You may now note "there is an ache here" or "at the present, there is an enjoyable feeling", etc.

A comparable type of technique that applies to both the foundations (body-focused) is a type of examining of the body; i.e. to look at the sensations, scanning up and down of the body & then watching the sensation flow through the body. Pay attention to what the sensation does.

By doing this type of mindfulness, a person can learn how to identify the tension in their body, and mindfully disarm the tension in the body, whether physical or psychological. A person is able to systematically loosen up and relax their entire body and mind by using mindfulness. By practicing this technique, people can begin to understand their body on a higher level than ever before.

Inspect the 3rd foundation, the mindfulness of psychological states. This covers images, fantasies, thoughts, ideas, etc. The focus is keeping an eye on how they are related to your current mind state, or desires. You can note "this idea has changed into this" or "all of a sudden I'm thinking about this".

Be aware of your thoughts, ideas and fantasies and note what they are. Let them run their course, however, if you find they are not benefitting you, or perhaps you are being dragged down by them in an endless loop, being mindful will give you the power to decide to break up these patterns.

Inspect the 4th and the final base, mindfulness of the consciousness. This may contain the state of mind, such as tiredness, energetic states, unfocused or focused states, feeling anxious or peaceful, etc.

Does your mind reject or desire something? Is a feeling like anger or greed dominating your mind? To help you become aware of your state of mind in the moment, you can ask yourselves questions like these.

Studying awareness is very interesting because it allows you to see how your thoughts and feelings change your momentary being. If the mind is full of life, it might make the mind happy and bright, however, it can also make the mind not able to concentrate on one thing. If the mind is full of life, but these thoughts are negative, it may make the person depressed.

The talent is to gently change or temper the state of the awareness, so that you may introduce appreciation when you feel dissatisfied, compassion when you feel depressed, or goodwill when you feel angry.

Taking a note: when being mindful you may note the things mentally or verbally. Perhaps noting the things mentally is considered to be the best method, since it builds concentration in reality. It comes down to personal preference. In the case of a monologue, you can study it just by describing each experience or sensation or noting every event. Doing this could be very useful in increasing insight with considering how the mind reacts to knowledge and words, but the practitioner has to be cautious not to get absorbed in a story.

Aim to put an effort towards quiet awareness and word-less awareness in the long run, where you are merely aware without using words or labels.

Letting go of any worrying states in the body and mind that occur is an essential part of all the 4 foundations. Being kind to yourself may be very difficult to practice, however it is an extremely important part of mindfulness meditation. To become upset at your inability to remain mindful will only draw you further out of a mindful state of being. The mind jumps into distress, fear, bewilderment, condemnation and confusion over and over again, which is a symbol that the mind is still inexperienced and wild. When you become more familiar with your body and mind, the mind and body doesn't act in the same way as in the past. In response to reoccurring emotions and problems, the body and mind will identify that what is being experienced is not new, and thus, these problems will dissolve much easier.

Some examples of people being mindful include:

A person lying on his/her right side & noticing the bones, sinews, muscles, body fluids, organs or even noticing relaxation, tension & added sensations.

In a sitting posture: A person is noting "in or out breathing", and other things like the muscles that were used to make the lungs bigger, the muscles that were getting used while "sitting", along with any mental feelings, hearing a noise, smelling a smell, sensations, thoughts, etc all while adding actions as they are being noticed.

A person walking up and down and noting his/her movements like: "slowing down, stopping, turning around and lifting foot, putting down foot, shifting weight", and so on, adding more delicate sensations and actions as they are noticed.

A person standing up and observing his/her muscles that are being used and how the muscle feels while standing up. Observing the different muscles the body uses to remain balanced. You may note and feel strain in the body, softness, coldness or heat, and general movements.

Chapter 18: External World And Breath Technique

This is an exercise where you notice the outside word and you realize how it comes in contact with your body. You'll also be focusing on your mindfulness, breathing, and external world and breath.

1. Sit comfortably and balanced on a cushion or chair and close your eyes if you feel comfortable doing so. You can allow your focus to fall on the floor or a few feet in front of you if you don't want to close your eyes.

2. Be aware of your body and the areas where it meets something solid, like your feet on the floor, perhaps the backs of your thighs against the chair, your behind, your back, and your shoulders resting where gravity has landed them.

3. Notice where your hands are touching, each other or your body, and notice the fabric on your clothes or skin, and maybe the air touching your skin. Notice your head resting on shoulders and your arms that are hanging from your shoulders. Allow your senses move to the sounds around you, not needing to think about them, but just allowing your attention to move from sound to sound. Maybe you can detect some scents or a lingering taste in your mouth. Let yourself just notice them.

4. Leave all of that and just focus on your breath, your natural breathing pattern. Bring all your awareness to the breath as it's moving in and out of your body, so the only movement you're aware of is the movement that's caused by your

breathing. Be aware of wherever it's easiest to detect your breaths: the nostrils, mouth, and the cool air and warm air entering your body.

5. As your thoughts come about, and they most likely will, just notice them and then let them move on. There's no need to chase them. Just bring your awareness back again to your breathing, your normal, natural breathing. You have nowhere else to be and nothing else to do. Just notice your breathing gently and practice this for a few moments.

6. Now expand that awareness outside of the body to the sounds that are around you and whatever emotions you have in your body. Notice any tensions, changes, looseness, tightness, or a sensation of floating. Sense the world around you as you feel your body resting in the chair or on the cushion. Open your eyes when you're ready to return to reality.

Chapter 19: Mindfulness In Your Daily Life

The mindfulness technique allows you to incorporate mindfulness into your daily tasks. It helps develop heightened awareness and it helps increase your appreciation of your daily task. If you go about your day on an auto-pilot, this activity will help increase your awareness of your daily tasks and activities. Here's how you can practice mindfulness in your daily life:

While brushing your teeth.

You can still practice mindfulness while doing a mundane task like brushing your teeth. Pay attention to the color of your toothpaste. Is it blue, red, or white? Do you see mint crystals? Does it have a jelly-like texture? Then, as you brush your teeth, pay attention to the sensations in your month/ Do you feel a warm sensation? Can you feel any mouth sores? How does the toothpaste taste? Is it sweet or is it minty? Notice how the brush feels on your teeth and your tongue. Take time to notice the motions of the brush. Then, as you wash your mouth with water, take time to notice how the water feels in your mouth. Is it warm or cold? Does it feel good? Do you feel any discomfort?

Doing this experience, you will help increase your awareness of your own tasks and experiences. Do this exercise every day and you'll be surprised with the result.

While working.

If you have an office job and you use a computer 99% of the time while you're in the office, then do "mindful typing". Before you start typing, take time to pay attention to your surroundings. What's the color of your personal computer? What's the color of your keyboard? What are the things on your desk aside from your computer? Do you see a pen, notebooks, or paper? Then, as you start typing, pay attention to your fingers. What are the sensations that you feel each time you hit your fingers on the keyboard? Are your fingers stiff? Do you feel pain or discomfort? Then, notice the sound of the keyboard as you press each key. Then, look at the screen and watch carefully as each letter starts appearing on your screen.

Many people avoid this mindfulness technique because they think that this will interfere with their work and will negatively affect their productivity, but it is actually the opposite. This practice will help improve your productivity and it allows you to work a lot faster than usual.

Opening a door

Whenever you open the door, take the time to examine the color and the texture of the door. Then, notice the color and the texture of the doorknob. How does it feel? Does it feel warm or cold? Can you feel the sweat in your palm as you touch the doorknob? Then, pay attention to the sound it makes when you twist the knob and open the door. This activity may look silly, but this will allow you to pay attention to simple day-to-day tasks such as opening the door.

People watching.

One way to practice meditation in your daily life is people watching. You can sit on a park bench and observe the people passing in front of you (just glance at them; do not stare). What's the color of that person's shirt, hair, or skin? Is he tall or short? How does he walk? Does it seem like he's in a hurry?

This exercise allows you to practice mindfulness in your daily life. This exercise also enhances your cognitive functions and observation skills that can improve your decision-making skills and productivity.

You can practice mindfulness in every aspect of your life. You can be mindful while you're watching TV, talking to your friends, drinking beer, cooking, and even while you are cleaning. When you practice mindfulness in everything that you do, you'll feel more immersed into your every experience. You feel more vibrant and alive. You also become more aware of the things that are happening around you. So, you won't feel that you're just someone who's drifting mindlessly through life.

Chapter 20: Loving Kindness

Loving kindness meditation is one of those things that is extremely effective but is quite hard to practice. This is because we're taught so many things as we grow up that we forget our real nature is to love things. The state of the outside world and the abuses we suffer turn us away from this.

Even worse, the quality of our self-talk that results from thwarted ambitions or goals results in us beating ourselves up over and over and the result is an epidemic of a lack of compassion.

This chapter is going to introduce the concept and practice of loving kindness meditation and the various elements of it. It is a very simple concept, but it is tough to put into practice, so take your time with it.

Self-compassion

Observe a child and you'll see a being that is full of self-compassion. Children are pretty vain creatures and assume themselves to be the center of the world, but this is a by-product of their ignorance. It is also the other side of the self-compassion coin. When have you ever known a child to hold back their feelings or suppress the expression of what they want?

In contrast, adults do this all the time. We jokingly refer to this as what adulthood is. However, this is a tragic state of affairs. It seems as if the attainment of great consciousness results in us sacrificing ourselves for things outside of us. We live and work to attain ideals which are placed upon us by our environment and end up placing our well-being last.

The self-help industry thrives on you putting yourself last. The problem doesn't lie in you not recognizing your potential or you are adopting the worries of other people, it lies squarely in you denying yourself kindness. I've mentioned self-talk previously in this book and how you should monitor it.

Your self-talk is just a small window into what your self-image is and, for most of us, it just isn't very good. No matter how successful you are in life, odds are that you call yourself an idiot or stupid once every day. Is it any wonder that you suffer from stress and anxiety?

While it's easy to say that you should be compassionate towards yourself, most of us have zero idea as to what this actually looks like. If I were to tell you to transmit love to those around you, can you figure out what I'm talking about? Probably not. It's not easy changing the habits of a lifetime.

The first step to practicing loving kindness with yourself is to reconcile with your past. You've made mistakes that have cost you and you're going to make mistakes that will continue to do so. Stop trying to aim for perfection and recognize yourself for the flawed being that you are. A lot of stress is caused by reminiscing over prior mistakes. You can't do a thing about them and yet we torture ourselves over them.

Practicing loving kindness is all about expansion. You begin with yourself, expand outward towards those closest to you, then to the world at large. However, it all starts with you. Accept yourself for who you are and accept what you have received in life thus far, even if you aren't happy with it. Stop striving so much and instead aim to relax into who you truly are.

The effectiveness of loving kindness is perhaps best illustrated by a story that originates from ancient India. A group of monks who had studied meditation under the Buddha decided to leave their monastery and travel to a forest to meditate. Why they thought this was a good idea isn't known. The point is that they did it.

Once they reached the forest and began meditating, they began hearing all kinds of howls and shrieks which terrified them. In a not so equanimous state, they packed up their things and fled back to the Buddha to seek his advice. The Buddha recommended that they send loving kindness towards these voices or spirits.

Armed with this information, the monks made their way back to the forest and sent loving kindness to these spirits through their practice. In a short while, these spirits were not only calmed but they even welcomed the monks and protected them from the elements.

While this story has a lot of mythology woven into it, there's no denying the wisdom that hatred and violence cannot be matched by further hatred and violence. Instead, it is love that cures it. Take the example of Lincoln, who referred to his enemies in the South as being human beings who erred instead of casting them as traitors or worse. This angered the self-appointed patriots who wanted him to vanquish his enemies, but

Lincoln's point was that by humanizing them, he was vanquishing them.

Formal Practice

As with the sitting meditation, you can record this in your own voice. Remember to pause at the end of the paragraphs to give yourself time to carry out the instructions. Also note that I have mentioned some sentences which imply the imparting of loving kindness to everything around you. If these phrases don't resonate with you, feel free to change them into something that does.

Assume your usual meditation posture and be thankful for taking the time to practice. Pat yourself on the back for doing so. Check in with yourself to see how you're feeling and the emotions that you have within you. As always, accept them for what they are and allow them to be. Simply observe and don't bother reacting.

Shift your awareness gently to your breathing and observe your breath. Live with every inhalation and exhalation, one at a time, without judgment or labels. Simply let your breath be as it is, knowing that everything is as it should be.

Slowly shift your awareness to your heart. Notice if you can feel any sensations of it at work. Don't strive to reach for these feelings if you can't feel anything. Simply remain at your level of consciousness and understand that wherever you are, this is perfectly fine. Accept the state of things.

Reflect on how you are subject to forces beyond your control. Like everything else in this world, you will grow old and fade away from this life. You were once born, and experienced life as did everyone else. You, like everyone and everything else on this planet, are a part of natural forces and you belong to them as much as they belong to you.

Can you see how much of a gift your life is? No matter the hardships you have faced, notice what a wonderful machine you've been given and what a miracle it is. Heart, brain and everything else working in unison to create your reality. You are subject to certain realities and the majority of them are good. Take some time to reflect on this.

Feel from your heart your endless capacity for boundless love and compassion. Can you feel a change in the sensations of your heart? Is it beating faster or slower? Do you feel anything within your chest? A change of temperature or any other sensation?

Can you feel how the love within you is as much a part of nature as is the sun, moon, stars and all of the life-giving qualities this world contains? Do you see how life is simply an expression of love and that without love, no life can exist? Notice how nothing separates you from any of this. All things are one.

Even if you cannot feel this emotion, do not judge yourself. Do not seek to label the experience as good or bad. It simply is. Keep focusing on your heart and its sensations.

Now, repeat the following phrases to yourself with as much love as you can muster, taking a few minutes to let each sink in. You may repeat this out loud or you can mentally recite them, it is your choice:

May I be happy.

May I be safe.

May I be compassionate towards everything.

Focus your attention to your loved ones next. Visualize them in your mind's eye and notice the sensations you experience in your heart. Repeat the following phrases:

May my loved ones be happy.

May my loved ones be safe.

May my loved ones be compassionate towards everything.

Move your consciousness to things in your vicinity, to the ones far beyond it. Extend your awareness to all the animals and other living things you share this world with and repeat:

May all living beings be happy

May all living beings be safe

May all living beings be compassionate towards everything.

Extend your awareness to people you are in conflict with. Extend your awareness to those you find unpleasant whether you know them personally or not. Repeat the following:

May all living beings be happy.

May all living beings be safe.

May all living beings be compassionate towards everything.

Spend some time focusing your awareness on those less fortunate, on those you feel sorry for, on those who are far more fortunate than you and extend your compassion and kindness to them. Give them the gift of your love.

Finally, bring your consciousness to focus on heavenly objects, the sun, the stars, the moon and the planets. Entire galaxies. Recognize how everything was created just for you to exist at this moment. Without any of them, you would not have received your gift of life. Extend your love to them wholeheartedly.

Return your focus to your breath and observe the sensations you feel. Allow them to be and do not judge yourself for anything. Do not label anything.

Open your eyes and take a minute to note your sensations.

Resistance

You may have noticed in the above meditation script that I kept mentioning the importance of not labeling or judging anything. Why was this? I mean, it's a loving kindness meditation, so where does judgment come into it?

Well, the truth is that you're not always going to feel very loving when you do this. Odds are you're going to think of yourself as being stupid for believing in this spiritual mumbo jumbo. We don't speak in this manner in public too often, so hearing it in private and then practicing it can be a bit too much for your mind to take.

This is perfectly fine and is a part of mindfulness practice. If anything, it is a benefit. You will become a lot more aware of the resistance and blocks within you. Extend your awareness to these blocks and allow them to be, however they are. It is very important that you allow these feelings to exist and recognize their importance.

These blocks are what are preventing you from experiencing happiness. These blocks are where your negative self-talk originates from and this is a great opportunity for you to explore your blocks. Exploring them is much the same as how you explored your emotions and thoughts in the previous chapter.

You can make this a part of your sitting meditation practice. But when else should you practice loving kindness? Well, just like every other form of mindfulness, there is a formal and informal practice associated with this. The formal practice is detailed above, and you can do this right after your sitting meditation ends. Spend around ten minutes practicing this. The more you do it the better, of course.

Informal loving kindness is simply treating everything in a compassionate manner and to adopt the other person's viewpoint as much as possible. If you find yourself unconsciously in an argument, well, now that your awareness has returned, put yourself in the other person's shoes and view the situation from their perspective.

Get outside of yourself as much as possible and do not hold back expressing your feelings with regards to anything. If you make a mistake, smile and forgive yourself. Show love wherever you get the opportunity to do so.

You'll find that the world will begin to reciprocate in kind.

Chapter 21: Mindfulness And Relationships

There are two things that you cannot do successfully if you don't learn to manage your stress levels and get them under control. You can't maintain successful relationships, and you can't be a successful leader. Being a leader is very different from being an **EFFECTIVE** leader. One title will be responsible for mediocre performance, but the other will head a team that is destined for success.

Mindfulness and Leadership

It's hard to be an effective leader when you're stressed. But then again, **how do you NOT feel stressed** when you've got such a major responsibility on your shoulders? Being a leader is not easy. The demands and the constantly changing environment makes you feel like you can never let your guard down. That you always need to be on your toes. Not only are you responsible for your work, but you are also responsible for inspiring, leading and motivating a team of individuals under you to be the very best that they can be every day at work to achieve the set goals. If your team is a ship, you (as the leader) are its captain, and the successful navigation of that ship depends on how well you do at the helm.

One of the toughest things about guiding and managing a team of people is working with all the different personalities and getting those personalities to work together effectively and successfully. Juggling the different relationship dynamics within that team successful so everyone can work as a cohesive unit. No two people are the same in a team, and therefore, there is no one-size-fits-all approach or solution that can be taken because of how different the people in a team can be. One approach may work for one person, but not necessarily work for another.

How Stress Impacts Your Leadership Style

Of all the different leaders and leadership styles out there, the most successful ones are the ones with the highest level of emotional intelligence (EI). Emotionally intelligent leaders are so good at what they do **because** they have mastered the art of mindfulness when they started practicing the five core principles of emotional intelligence. These five principles are **self-awareness, self-regulation, motivation, social skills, and empathy**. All five EI skills require some degree of mindfulness, and that is exactly why these leaders have succeeded where others fall short.

One thing that successful leaders have in common is that they **don't** have chronic stress to deal with on top of everything else. Oh, they certainly do have their fair share of stress. They've simply learned how to manage it better so it doesn't affect their performance. Dealing with chronic stress is going to profoundly affect your ability to be a leader because of the way it affects your brain in the following ways:

• **By Diminishing Your Memory Power** - The hippocampus is the part of the brain responsible for turning short-term memories into long-term ones. When you're dealing with chronic stress, the hippocampus is going to shrink over time, making you more forgetful. Being forgetful means you might miss important deadlines, information, and possible client meetings. Even overlook vital information that you forgot to pass along to your team. That's going to reflect poorly on your leadership abilities.

• **By Diminishing Motivation** - Neurotransmitters is the brain's fundamental way that our brain cells communicate. Chronic stress is going to cause a problem by creating an imbalance in these important chemicals. When there's an imbalance, the likelihood of becoming anxious, depressed, and listless increases while your lack of motivation as a result of those conditions. When was the last time you looked up to a leader who was not motivated?

• **By Amplifying Anxiety** - If you're already anxious in general, chronic stress is only going to amplify that. When that happens, cortisol is produced in excess, creating an imbalance in the brain's chemicals. These are called neurotransmitters, and an imbalance here is going to cause the amygdala (the right or flight center) to go into high alert mode. A leader who is anxious and prone to irrational reactions, as a result, will never make an effective leader.

• **By Shortening Your Fuse** - A quick-tempered leader is not going to last very long. No team can successfully thrive under that kind of leadership style. When the amygdala is in overdrive, the pre-frontal cortex can't function optimally the way that it should. The pre-frontal cortex is responsible for a lot of the reflection, thinking, and reaction that goes on. When that's disrupted by stress, it gives you a shorter fuse and you easily "snap" at the slightest trigger. Not an effective leadership style at all.

- **By Hampering Your Decision-Making Abilities** - Not being able to think and reflect before you react (pre-frontal cortex again) means you're not thinking clearly enough to make rational, thoughtful decisions. When faced with stressful situations, a leader who is **already stressed** as it is might make the situation worse when they're not thinking clearly enough to make the right decision. Leaders who don't make good decisions are eventually going to be the downfall of their team.

Using Mindfulness to Create A Positive Work Environment

Any successful manager or leader would know that if you want to be the best out of your employees, there is one thing that needs to be a constant in any situation – **a positive environment.** For a team to work together to achieve success with their leader, every member of the team needs to feel encouraged, motivated and most of all, happy to be there and to be doing what they are doing. Since you are the leader, it is safe to say that this responsibility will fall on your shoulders. You must be mindful of the kind of environment you're creating and how it affects productivity levels.

Mindfulness is once again going to be a useful skill to possess. Aside from cultivating the right professional environment where others can thrive in, Kabat-Zinn believes that mindfulness is necessary for leadership for two reasons. The first is so you can see things for what they are. The second is so you can be non-judgmental and pay attention to what's happening in the present. Non-judgmental being the key term here since what you're trying to create right now is an environment of positivity. Here are some examples of how mindfulness can be used to foster a dynamic work environment and improve relationships among the team:

• **Using Mindfulness to Engage** - When you engage with your team, go the extra mile, and make a connection with each member of your team. Don't connect for the sake of doing so, but build a meaningful connection, that shows your team you genuinely care about them and their welfare, not just because it is part of your job to do so. Be present when you engage with them, and never do it when you're preoccupied or feeling pressed for time. When you engage, you need to commit to being in the moment. Be mindful of how they feel and **listen** to what they tell you. This will give you insight into what changes need to be made for the better.

• **Better Communication** - Communication is one of the most important traits you need to have if you are going to become an effective leader and manage a team of successful individuals. A leader needs to be emotionally available, and mindfulness is how you remain present in any conversation you engage in. You must be able to communicate in a way that leaves no doubt to your team what you expect from them and what needs to be done, which means you're going to have to focus and be present to avoid communicating the wrong message.

• **Practice Empathy** - A successful leader is one who can practice empathy and compassion with sincerity. How? By being mindful of how emotions and actions can affect performance. Remember, people are more acute at spotting insincerity than you think, no matter how good of an actor you think you are. Be mindful that your team members are people with emotions and feelings, put yourself in their shoes and try to imagine what they would be feeling.

• **Set an Example** - An effective manager is one that can lead by example. When you're mindful that your team is watching what you do, what motivates you to remain mindful and vigilant about what's happening in the present. Be someone that your team can look up to, admire and respect, and show them the right thing to do by doing the right thing first. If you insist on your team being punctual, for example, then you need to ensure that you punctual too. If you remain calm and cool in stressful situations, your team will do the same.

• **Being Mindful About Body Language** - Communication goes far beyond the words that you say out loud. Some of the most powerful forms of communication come in the form of body language. A lot of ineffective leaders overlook this point, and they're not paying attention to how their body language affects the people around them. Your words may be able to tell a lie, but your body language is far more revealing than you could ever imagine. What is said in those unspoken and nonverbal cues will be a big clue as to how that person is feeling. As a leader, you must be mindful of this nonverbal element to your communication and make a conscious effort to pay attention. Not just to your body language, but to the language of the people you work with too. Your staff will be looking towards your body language as a leader, and a successful leader is one that projects an air of confidence, honesty, and trustworthiness every day.

• **Mindful Listening** - Paying mindful attention with all your senses engaged means you need to **actively listen**. If you were an employee, would you want a leader who is open and willing to listen to your needs? Or a leader who just listens but dismisses it as soon as you've brought it up. You are the one they will go to when they feel something needs to be improved, and when employees feel that their leader is taking their every concern seriously, no matter how small it may be, and taking steps to fix it, they will feel appreciated.

Mindfulness and Relationships

Relationships are built and developed over time. You may be good at your job, but your "people skills" could be holding you back from that promotion you've been eyeing for months now. If your people skills are lacking, aspiring to a leadership position one day is going to be nothing more than a dream. Without the ability to form meaningful relationships, both your professional and personal life will feel like a constant struggle.

To build strong relationship bonds, it will help if you're naturally curious, to begin with. Within the mindfulness context, curiosity is a good thing. It is the very thing that is going to help build a strong relationship foundation because it starts with a genuine desire to connect with someone else and what they may be going through in their lives. This doesn't mean you need to ask nosy, prying, or invasive questions, but it is more about asking the **right kind of questions** that encourage others to open to you. The more we encourage our curiosity, the better our chances of forging bonds and connections with people from all walks of life, even those which are vastly different from our own. People we wouldn't normally connect with, which is going to give you an

advantage when you're a leader.

Whether professional or personal, being mindful is the key to helping any relationship you forge blossom. The ability to be present will lead you to become more compassionate, open, and self-aware about how you respond to others. Being mindful is the key to relationship health since it directs your attention towards the kind of thoughts you have about these relationships and conscious about how you react because of those thoughts. For example, if you were being particularly judgmental toward someone, you might treat them harshly or with less compassion than you would. When they come to you for advice, and perhaps as a shoulder to cry on, having these judgmental thoughts might cause you to react on autopilot in a way that makes them feel worse.

The Journal of Human Sciences and Extension published a meta-analysis study that revealed that those who were mindful had happier, more satisfying and fulfilling relationships. These are even more reasons why mindfulness is good for your relationships:

• **It Minimizes Your Tendency to Be Negative** - When your mindfully aware of how your words and actions affect others, it makes you think before you react. Studies that were carried out on subjects who practiced 8 to 10 weeks of mindfulness showed a significant change in the way the brain regulated emotions. The amygdala tendency to overreact was diminished over the course of those 10 weeks, making it easier to put a stop to destructive patterns of behavior. Being less negative means you're more open and accepting of others, regardless of their shortcomings. When others feel less judged by you, they're more open to forging a genuine connection instead.

• **It Improves the Way You Regulate Emotions** - Because mindfulness strengthens the prefrontal cortex and subsequently its connection to the amygdala, you're able to get a better handle on your emotions. Even if something the other person says or does happens to trigger an emotional reaction from you, you're less likely to lose your cool or explode in an emotional manner. You start making a conscious effort to remind yourself that everyone expresses themselves differently and there's no reason to get worked up over it. When you practice tolerance, it makes it easier to have effective conversations.

• **It Minimizes the Potential for Ego to Get in The Way** - Ego can be a very powerful force that resides within all of us and a barrier that keeps mindful relationships from taking place. If we let our egos make the decisions instead of our hearts, that's where a lot of problems start to happen. When you let ego take the driver seat, it can cause you to manipulate your relationships, and be the main reason for a lot of arguments, fights, depressions, aggression, passive-aggressiveness, revenge, self-doubt, distrust, intolerance, blame, competition, put down your partner and even disrespectful gestures. All of these negative qualities will eventually cause your relationship to deteriorate and breakdown over time.

• **It Helps You Stay Calm** - The ability to stay come is going to be your biggest asset in determining a positive outcome for any conversation that you have. Especially the difficult ones. This is where mindfulness comes into play. During a particularly difficult conversation, you can sometimes struggle to maintain your composure or to keep your voice calm and friendly when you're not aware of the direction your thoughts and emotions are taking. Until it's too late and things start to quickly escalate out of control. When that happens, others will start to sense all that nervous and tense energy that is happening and find it hard to keep their emotions in check too. Whenever you feel yourself start to get more emotional, mindfulness will be the one that leads you to hit the pause button, take a 10-15-minute break and then come back and revisit the issue when you're much calmer.

• **It Lets You Apologize Mindfully** - An apology is supposed to serve two purposes. The first is to show remorse over your actions, and the second is to acknowledge that your actions may have caused someone else a lot of hurt and pain. Apologizing and saying all the right words is easy, but apologizing **mindfully** requires that you think about what you're saying and say it with emotion and feeling. Mindful apologies are more meaningful because of the sincerity and genuine feeling that is involved. Everyone makes mistakes along the way, but the difference lies in the way that you handle what happens after those mistakes have been made, how you restore the harmony and the trust in your relationship, and how you let others know you are genuinely sorry for what happened.

• **It Makes You More Forgiving** - Getting angry is easy. But forgiveness? Well, that's a different story. It takes great inner strength to forgive and be the bigger person, but this is something you cannot achieve without the ability to mindfully process your emotions. It is a choice that you alone must make. It helps to remind yourself that this is someone you love and that alone should be enough of a reason for forgiveness. **"Forgiveness is something that is attributed to the strong,"** that was what Gandhi said. Forgiveness is one of the most powerful tools you could possess to make letting things go much easier. Not only will you eventually gain the ability to forgive others over time when you let go of your ego, but you'll also learn to forgive yourself. You'll learn acceptance, and you'll learn how to be much happier when you let go of all the anger that resides within you.

• **It Encourages the Use of Positive Speech** - Which is especially beneficial in a romantic relationship. Learning to talk about the difficult things can be much easier if both you adopt the approach to only use positive language during the conversation. Being mindful about how damaging and powerful the wrong choice of words can be let's you think carefully before you speak instead of just blurting out the first thing that comes to mind. Phrases such as **I hear what you're saying and I value what you have to say or I know this is difficult to talk about, but I'm here to support you and we can work through this together** are examples of some great positive language that can be used to help control the conversation and steer it in the right direction. It minimizes the chances of things escalating and getting out of hand. You're also less likely to experience those moments when you wish you could take back what you said.

Chapter 22: Positive Mind, Positive Life

Psychologists divide our thoughts into two systems: the unconscious thought system and the conscious thought system. As the name states, the unconscious thought system consists of the thoughts that occur without our control, while the conscious thought system consists of the thoughts that we control. The unconscious thought system takes less energy to run than the conscious thought system. Your brain is always trying to work at optimum energy levels, so it will automatically look for thought patterns that are already established in order to use less energy.

The key is to ensure that even your automatic, unconscious thoughts are positive ones. The manner in which your brain decides which thoughts will become automatic is that it looks at the relative weight of those thoughts, in other words, the seeming importance, and the duration of the thoughts, that is, the time that you spend focused on those thoughts. If a thought seems to be important to you, based on how much attention you pay to it, as well as how long you spend ruminating that thought, your brain will classify it as a thought of high importance and it will automatically refer back to that thought regularly and without your conscious action.

This same concept applies regardless of whether the thought is positive or negative because your brain cannot distinguish between the two. Awareness of your thoughts and paying attention to your internal conversation is the key to starting to rewire your brain from negative automatic thought patterns to positive automatic thought patterns. The root of personal power is to acknowledge and redirect thoughts where necessary.

A good exercise to start the shift toward positive automatic thinking is to schedule positive thinking time. Write down some questions that could only have positive outcomes, such as "what am I grateful for today?" and schedule time to answer those questions three times per day. The more your brain starts to recognize that there are these different thought patterns that you are spending more time on, it will decide that these must be important so they should be filed under automatic thoughts (Burchard, 2014).

In this chapter, we reflect back on the concept of the external world being a mirror for your internal world. If we wish to see positivity, then we need to be positive and embody a positive disposition. At the outset, it should be clarified that positive thinking is not unrealistic thinking nor can it be said that people that are generally positive are naive about the realistic possibilities of bad things happening that cannot be controlled. It is also not to say that if we achieve a state of positive thinking that only good things will ever happen to us. Essentially, we need to ask ourselves if we are finding negative things because that is perhaps where our thought focus lays and if we switch that up and decide to look for positive things, we will undoubtedly find more of them.

Let's use a very simple example, if I woke up this morning and told myself that my focus for the week was going to be llamas, then I will be consciously seeking the word <u>llama,</u> pictures of llamas or anything that represents a llama. I am going to see the references to llamas that week because I'm looking for them. They were probably there the week before too, but I wasn't looking for them then.

The same can be said for someone who wakes up with the mindset that they are expecting negative things to appear that week. They will absolutely be affirmed in that because a search for negative things is their focus. The negative things were there before too, but they weren't as noticeable because that wasn't your focus. As your focus shifts, so does your reality because your reality is built from the things you see.

What Is Positive Thinking?

The essence of positive thinking is to expect good things to happen and when bad things happen not to let that override your search for good. It is a mental and emotional attitude. If you are building a positive mindset, you will not allow life's occasional downturns to knock you off your path. They are simply a pebble in the road to be stepped over. Certainly, some pebbles are larger than others, but with a positive-thinking mindset, you will be secure in the knowledge that there is always a way around the obstacle. Your focus is on the other side of the obstacle, not the obstacle itself.

A person with a positive mindset will naturally see the good in people. Again, this is not to say that one should ignore any negative energy at the preclusion of the existence of good energy but negative energy from a person can be acknowledged and moved on from, it does not need to be your focus. A positive person will also naturally want to help others to grow and better themselves, understanding that the growth of others is always the foundation of our own growth. If you have ever met someone that always has a problem for every solution, without even having tried the solution, that person does not yet have a positive mindset.

In a relationship aspect, positive thinking will allow you to move on from a relationship, taking with you the lessons you have learned about yourself and build on that to create a stronger relationship with someone else in the future. If you were unable to think this way, you may continuously choose people who are not suited for you because you are perhaps trying to correct what you believe you did wrong. The truth is, however, that if a relationship has expired, it is not meant for you and the best thing you can do for all concerned is use its lessons together with positive thinking to continue on the journey to find the right person for you.

The best way to guide yourself toward positive thinking is to attempt to identify something good about every situation. This technique of seeking the positive will eventually become an automatic behavior for you (Sasson, n.d.).

Science Agrees

Barbara Fredrickson is a psychologist from the University of North Carolina. She specializes in the field of positive psychology. She has written a paper which is being cited and further researched significantly at other institutes. The premise of Fredrickson's research is that positive thinking is not a fluffy term used to describe people who smile all the time, but it is, in fact, a very real and quantifiable psychological outlook that can have far-reaching effects on a person's emotional wellbeing, family, career and even health.

Fredrickson's initial research involved exposing three control groups to video clips which were designed to elicit specific emotions. One group were exposed to negative emotional clips, the second group was exposed positive emotional clips and the third were exposed to video clips that were neutral.

She then gave all of the participants a piece of paper with the words "I would like to..." written on it and they were asked to complete the phrase with as many items as possible relating to the emotions which were elicited in the video clips.

The group that was exposed to the positive emotions consistently were able to write down far more examples of what they would like to do than the neutral or negative group. This research reflects that positive emotions significantly open up the number of possibilities that we can imagine for ourselves whereas negative emotions severely narrow our scope of what is possible.

This extends into our skill set. Positive people who regularly find ways to promote positive emotions in their life will tend to build a larger skill set than people who focus on negative emotions. This in turn helps positive people to achieve success which increases positive thoughts and emotions in a cycle (Clear, n.d.).

Conclusion

Thank you again for downloading this book.

This book has shown you how to practice mindfulness as well as the perks of consistent mindfulness practice. With mindfulness, you will better appreciate your life and be able to live in the present. You will be more peaceful as a result, and many aspects of your life will improve greatly, including your mental and physical health.

Thank you, and good luck!

www.ingramcontent.com/pod-product-compliance
Lightning Source LLC
Chambersburg PA
CBHW072011070526
44583CB00015B/1427